W9-BCJ-505

Advance Praise for *Selling the Wheel*

(continued from back jacket)

"What a fantastic read! This book will make you laugh, think, and by the time you are done, you will thoroughly understand the fundamentals of building a world-class organization."
—Jerry Marterella, Vice-President, Computer Sciences Corporation, Consulting and Systems Integration

"The Wheel in the story is symbolic of every product and service in the world today. In my twenty-five-plus years of sales management, I have to say this book is without a doubt the easiest to read and the most enjoyable—yet it delivers concepts that are essential to salespeople everywhere. I highly recommend it."
—Don Herring, Vice-President, Standard Motor Products, Inc.

"*Selling the Wheel* is fast-paced and a lot of fun to read—even as it offers a wealth of information about choosing the right way to sell for your kind of customers. If you're in business today, you've got to read *Wheel*."
—Jake J. Antonio III, Vice-President of Sales, Hill-Rom /A Hillenbrand Company

"*Selling the Wheel* is a clever story about sales, a story that teaches concepts better than a standard textbook could ever do. The plot rolls along—as if on wheels!—gathering speed all the way to the end. You won't want to put it down. *Wheel* would be a discussion-provoking text for marketing classes at any level."
—Lois Herr, Marketing & Public Affairs, Elizabethtown College

"*Selling the Wheel* offers a clear, concise, fun-to-read understanding of how to approach your customer and your market. It is a crucial tool for anyone in sales, a roadmap for a rookie and a fresh perspective for even the most seasoned rep! The story is so good that I recommend it to anyone who wants to sell more, quicker."
—Charlie Alvarez, Vice-President, Corporate Development, Physicians Sales & Service, World Medical

SELLING
THE
WHEEL

Choosing the <u>Best</u> Way to Sell for You,
Your Company, and Your Customers

JEFF COX
and
HOWARD STEVENS

Simon & Schuster
New York London Sydney Singapore

SIMON & SCHUSTER
Rockefeller Center
1230 Avenue of the Americas
New York, NY 10020

Copyright © 2000 by Jeff Cox
Illustrations copyright © 2000 by David Cain
All rights reserved, including the right of reproduction
in whole or in part in any form.
SIMON & SCHUSTER and colophon are registered
trademarks of Simon & Schuster, Inc.

Designed by Sam Potts
Manufactured in the United States of America

1   3   5   7   9   10   8   6   4   2

Library of Congress Cataloging-in-Publication Data
Cox, Jeff
Selling the wheel : choosing the *best* way to sell for you, your company,
and your customers / Jeff Cox and Howard Stevens.
p.   cm.
1. Selling—Fiction. I. Stevens, Howard. II. Title.
PS3553.O9196S45   2000
813'.54—dc21   99-38449
CIP
ISBN 0-684-85600-X

For Sue and for Sally

SELLING
THE
WHEEL

Introduction

Selling the Wheel is written as a story. Yet everything said in these pages about salespeople and customers is derived from empirical research conducted over more than twenty-five years.

Our research began in the mid-1970s, and it continues today. It's comprised of data collected on 250,000 salespeople, more than 8,500 corporate sales forces, and interviews with over 100,000 actual customers who rated the quality of the salespeople and sales forces serving them.

As our firm analyzed the data, we made some interesting discoveries. For one thing, we learned that there is no such thing as the perfect salesperson who is universally effective with all customers. Indeed, we found that most so-called sales superstars are typically very ineffective when it comes to the nuts-and-bolts selling that is the essence of many business-to-business sales. In fact, the strengths that make one salesperson successful in one selling situation might turn into weaknesses if that salesperson is placed in a different situation, dealing with different customer needs.

Customers are, of course, the key to everything in sales. So we decided that in order to make sense of our growing mountain of data, we would sort it according to the two most critical criteria relevant *to customers*.

First, *the complexity of the purchase decision* (that is, whether the sale can be made in one or two contacts with the customer, or whether the sale requires an involved effort over an extended period of time).

Second, *the experience and expertise of the customer* in making the purchase of the item being sold (that is, whether the customer is familiar with the product or service and can competently buy it and use it without much support, or whether the customer needs a lot of help from the seller's salespeople).

Sorted in such fashion, the data revealed profiles of four specific types of salespeople—who have different personal career drives, different personalities, and who need different kinds of skills because they must use different approaches to finding customers and making sales. Each type could be effective, but only when matched to customers' needs.

We further observed a broad range of implications affecting practically all aspects of market strategy—from market entry and withdrawal to pricing and profitability, new product development, corporate image, sales force compensation, and just about everything else.

In 1998, we teamed up with Jeff Cox—a writer with whom we have worked on several occasions and the coauthor of some well-known, best-selling business books—to present the essence of this material simply and creatively, yet accurately. The result is *Selling the Wheel*.

We hope you enjoy the book, because it is written to be enjoyable. More important, we hope you identify yourself and your company in this story, because every salesperson and every company has a place on the Wheel of Sales. And understanding that place is critical to your success and that of your company.

As the business world enters a new millennium, competition has never been more intense—yet the tools for waging the competitive struggle are becoming fewer rather than more plentiful. Consider the changes that have taken place in the last three decades.

In the 1970s, when our firm, the H. R. Chally Group, was founded, many long-held tenets of American management were being challenged and overturned. Japanese corporations in particular were gaining share with products that were of higher quality, as perceived by the customer, and were also lower in cost. Quality improvement, then, became the means to a competitive advantage.

Similarly, in the 1980s, the spread of powerful computer technologies made it possible to engineer, introduce, and distribute new products in less time. Technology also made it possible to provide those products with higher-quality service and support. And, defensively, if a competitor introduced a superior product, you could reverse-engineer it and bring a comparable offering to the market much more quickly. So a product offering quality and lower cost was no longer enough to gain a competitive edge. You also needed excellent service.

In the 1990s, the spread of computer networks, the rise of global manufacturing, and automated or outsourced service improvements made it possible to downsize workforces and create leaner, more-efficient corporate organizations. This also meant that buyers could lower their own overhead expenses, which enabled them to offer lower prices to their own customers . . . but to do so required outsourcing back to their vendors much of the added values that can only be provided by a vendor's sales and service people.

But now, none of these—not quality, technology, or a lean organization—is a competitive advantage. They are now merely the qualifications for entry into the marketplace. If you have them, you're a contender; if you don't, you're history.

Today, the single most potent resource for gaining a competitive edge is not the product being sold or the guarantees you attach: it is the quality of the sales force selling that product. In fact, we are now seeing that the closer products in the marketplace move toward parity with one another, the better the sales force has to become if the seller's company is to succeed.

On that note, enjoy the book, learn from it—and if you'd like to learn more or apply our principles and services to your company, look up www.chally.com on the Net.

Howard Stevens
Dayton, Ohio
A.D. 2000

Part One

THE WHEEL
REVOLUTION

Once upon a time, a long, long time ago, way back in the days of the Pharaohs of ancient Egypt, there lived a guy named Max.

One day, Max was traveling on business, and he had a layover between caravans. Stuck with time on his hands, Max got to talking to a few of the locals, and they told him all about this big Pyramid that was under construction—it was the largest stone structure ever attempted in the history of the world.

"Where is it?" Max asked them.

"It's right on the edge of town," they said. "You can't miss it."

"What the heck," said Max, "maybe I'll go have a look."

So he rented a camel, rode it to the edge of town, and sure enough, there in the distance were the sloping foundations of what would someday be the very first Pyramid. And everywhere Max looked, he saw thousands of sweaty workers cutting big, heavy stones with hammers and chisels, and then dragging the huge stones into place. To move the heaviest of stones, they had elephants, dozens of them, but even with the help of elephants the work was hot, backbreaking, and slow.

Man, it's going to take them forever to build this thing, thought Max.

Impressed though he was with what he saw, he was very glad that he wasn't working there.

When Max got home, he couldn't stop thinking about that huge Pyramid and all those workers dragging the stones around. He even had a dream one night that he was one of the stone-dragging team, toiling in the sun, and after tossing and turning for half the night, he awakened with a terrible thirst.

He got out of bed to get a drink of water—and lo! He had the most brilliant idea he'd ever had in his life.

As he sipped his drink of water, he thought about his idea. He went back to bed, thought about it some more, and the more he thought, the more he was convinced that his idea was really something.

At last, Max nodded off to dreamland, but in the morning when he woke up, his idea was still with him. And it still seemed brilliant to him. So he went downstairs to the workshop he had in a spare room at the back of his house and he set to it.

Years later, after many disappointments and failures, Max had done it. He had turned his idea into a real thing. Very proud of his accomplishment, he rolled it out of the workshop and into the kitchen to show his wife.

"Look, Minnie!" he said. "Look what I've invented!"

"What the heck is that?" his wife asked.

"It's the Wheel!" said Max.

"It's the *what*?"

"The Wheel. This is what I've been working on all these years."

"Yeah? What's it do?"

"What's it do? You just watch!" And Max rolled the Wheel across the kitchen floor. "See, it goes 'round and 'round!"

"That's . . . interesting. Does it do anything else?"

"Well, no, that's pretty much it. But, Minnie, I think the Wheel could turn out to be a very useful thing."

"What makes you think that?"

"Because people won't have to *drag* things the way they always have. With the aid of the Wheel, you see, heavy objects can be made to *roll*."

"So?" asked his wife.

"Don't you get it? The Wheel is going to make it possible to move things much more quickly—and with far less effort! People will get more work done in less time!"

"Well, it sounds good," said Minnie, trying not to look skeptical.

"And you know what else?" said Max. "The Wheel is going to make us lots of money!"

"Oh?"

"Someday, millions of people all over the world will use the Wheel. And we will own the patent!"

"Uh-huh. Well, that's nice, dear. You keep at it, and let me know when we're rich."

Max did keep at it. He built more and more Wheels. He filled his whole workshop with them—and each Wheel he built was better and more refined.

One evening, Minnie came into the workshop. She stood perplexed amidst Max's vast inventory of Wheels, and asked, "So, um, how's it going?"

"Not bad," said Max. "Take a look at this one. See? It's rounder!"

"Very nice, dear."

"And take a look at this!" said Max, holding up a thick wooden pole. "I call it the Axle."

"Oh? And what does an Axle do?"

"Well, you see, Minnie, with an Axle, I can join together two Wheels, one on each end, and place the object to be moved in the middle! This is eminently more practical than using one Wheel by itself—and just think of it—I can sell twice as many Wheels!"

"I'm glad you brought that up," said his wife.

"Brought what up?"

"*Selling* these things. It seems to me that if we're going to get rich, you're going to have to go out and *sell* these Wheels of yours, aren't you?"

"Sell? Me? Minnie, the Wheel is a brilliant invention! One does not have to *sell* brilliant inventions; brilliant inventions sell themselves!"

"Uh-huh. Well, I haven't been seeing the Wheels rolling out the door on their own. I don't think they know *how* to sell themselves. I think you're going to have to do it for them."

This suggestion gave Max a modest anxiety attack. Because while he now knew a great deal about Wheels, he knew almost nothing about selling.

"You just wait, Minnie. When word of the Wheel gets around, and the idea catches on, there'll be people lined up outside our door begging me to sell them a Wheel."

Weeks went by, but nobody lined up outside Max's door.

Finally, Max could not fit any more Wheels into the workshop. He wanted to start storing them in the living room, but Minnie laid down the law.

"Absolutely not!" his wife said. "You've got to get rid of some of these Wheels. Either start selling them or roll them into the river!"

At last Max had to face reality. After grumping about the house for a few hours, he picked out his two roundest Wheels, rolled them into the street, attached them to his best Axle, and pushed his contraption through the neighborhood.

"Look," Max would say to anyone who would give him the time, "aren't these terrific? I call them 'Wheels.' They're my own invention. You see, with Wheels, you don't have to drag things, you can—hey, wait a minute! Come back!"

Unfortunately for Max, no one was interested. After weeks of pushing his Wheels up one street and down the next, knocking on doors, introducing himself, explaining these great things called Wheels—nothing! Nobody wanted them.

Some even laughed at Max's suggestion that they might want to purchase Wheels of their own.

"You want money? For *those*? Ha! Ha! Ha-ha-ha!"

It was embarrassing, even humiliating, for poor Max. He began to doubt that he could even give away his Wheels. Finally, very depressed and disappointed, he turned and rolled them toward home.

"All that time and effort I put in! And for what?" he asked aloud as he removed the Wheels from their Axle.

Disgusted, he gave one of the Wheels a kick. It rolled to the wall, bumped it hard enough to make a crack in the plaster, and toppled over. *Plop.*

Minnie looked at her husband and felt bad. She sat down with him on the sofa, put her hand on his arm.

"I can't believe it!" Max lamented. "Here I come up with what might possibly be one of the greatest inventions ever, and nobody wants it!"

"Max, there are millions of people in the world. Surely *some* of them must have a use for the Wheel."

"But how do I find them? And if I find them, how do I sell it to them?"

Minnie slowly shook her head. "I don't know."

They both thought for a moment.

Then Minnie said, "Hey, what about the Oracle?"

"What, you mean Ozzie the Oracle? What about him?"

"He knows everything about everything—politics, history, the

mysteries of the universe. He must know something about marketing and sales. Why don't we go talk to him?"

"Aw, Minnie, come on! It's a pain in the neck getting out to
see him. He lives in the middle of nowhere, and you've got to
bring him a burnt offering, and . . . I'm not so sure he really
knows *everything*."

"Well, he does know a lot," said Minnie. "Surely he can give
you a few tips on how to sell your invention. Besides, I'm not sure
what else to do."

In truth, Max did not know what to do either. Finally, he got
to his feet. "All right, all right. Let's go hear what the old codger
has to say."

In those days, if you wanted to know something beyond the realm of everyday experience, you went to see the Oracle. Every town had one. For the price of a burnt offering, you could ask any question and the Oracle would tune in to the infinite and tell you what was what.

So Max packed up some Wheels and Axles, put them on a donkey, and he and Minnie made the tortuous journey to visit the Oracle. They left the city and followed the narrow path along a river, up through a winding canyon of sheer cliffs, and into some arid mountains where nothing grew except bugs and snakes. They kept going until they came to the yawning mouth of a dark and forbidding cave.

Max and Minnie peered inside but saw nobody. Finally, summoning their courage, they stepped into the cave. When their eyes adjusted, they detected a pile of sticks off to one side and, in the center of the cave, the cold ashes of a fire.

Going on what others had said, Max built a fire from the sticks while Minnie skewered their offering. They put it over the fire and waited. Slowly the cave filled with the smoke of burning meat that drifted back into its farthest reaches—and suddenly there appeared, as if from thin air, an old bald man with a long white beard.

The old man snatched the skewer from the fire, blew on it, then took a little nibble.

"Mmmm. Not bad. What is this?"

"Roasted goat," said Minnie.

"Tasty."

The old man sat down on a rock, polished off the remainder of the burnt offering, then sighed and announced in a rather bored, official tone, "Greetings and welcome to my cave. I am Ozzie the Oracle, knower of all things knowable and some that are not. And you are . . . ?"

"This is my wife, Minnie. And my name is Max. I'm the inventor the Wheel."

"The what?"

"The Wheel. One of these round things I brought with me."

"Those? You're kidding. I thought they were giant bagels."

"No, they're made of stone, and they roll back and forth like . . . well, here, let me show you."

Max removed the Wheels and Axles from the donkey, assembled them, and proceeded to demonstrate. But the Oracle, though initially curious, soon began to watch with growing impatience.

"Okay, okay," said the Oracle, "I get the idea. What's your problem?"

"See, I'm convinced that Wheels have a great future," said Max, "but I haven't been able to sell them to anyone."

As Max went on to explain the ordeal of going around the neighborhood and having everyone either laugh at him or run away, the Oracle stroked his beard and thought. Minnie took out paper, ink, and a quill in case he said something worth writing down.

At last, the Oracle said, "Max, you've got to keep in mind that people have been getting along just fine without the Wheel for millions of years."

"What do you mean by that?"

"The world does not know that it needs the Wheel. Just because you've invented it doesn't mean the world wants it."

"So you think I should give up?" asked Max. "You think I should throw the Wheel on the scrap heap of history?"

"No, no," said the Oracle. "In fact, I predict that the Wheel will indeed have a bright future. But to find the right way to sell it, you have to start by answering the basic, bedrock questions."

"What are those?"

"Well, the first one is: Who are your customers?"

"That's the problem," said Max. "I don't have any customers yet."

"But who is a potential customer for the Wheel?"

"Why . . . everyone!"

"No, not really. Maybe someday everyone will own a Wheel— or even three or four of them. But not today. So think, in the next few months, who is *most likely* to become a customer?"

"Beats me," said Max.

"Okay, if you don't know who your customers are, let me ask you the second bedrock question: Who are your competitors?"

"My competitors? I don't have any of those either," said Max. "The Wheel is unique, the first product of its kind. We have no competitors."

"Oh, yes you do," said the Oracle. "Your competition is the existing technology—*technology that is already in place*. I'm talking about all of the different ways of moving things from one place to another."

Max thought for a moment. "You mean like camels. Horses. Elephants. Big sweaty guys with strong backs. And sledges."

You have to understand that in those days, B.W. (before the Wheel), people would use a sledge to move the very heaviest objects. A sledge was a platform on top of a couple of skids or runners—kind of like a sled, even though they did not have much snow in Max's part of the world. Anyway, they would put the big, heavy object to be moved onto a sledge, hitch up some kind of beast to pull it, and they would drag it to wherever they needed this huge, heavy thing to be.

"Yeah, I guess you're right," said Max. "The Wheel does have competitors. It even has a number of them."

"All right, here's the third question: Why do your customers—or your potential customers—want what you are selling? That is, what does the Wheel do *better* than the competitive alternatives?"

"Well, with a Wheel you can move things a lot faster and with a lot less work," said Minnie.

"And you can move them cheaper, too, because you don't need as many camels or elephants or workers to pull things using a Wheel," said Max.

"Ah, but there's something else you're selling," said the Oracle.

"What's that?"

"Opportunity. You're conceivably selling the opportunity to move things and do things that could never have been moved or done before the Wheel."

"True," said Max.

"Okay," said the Oracle, "now let's go back to the first question: Who are your customers?"

"People who need to move heavy stuff faster, easier, and cheaper," said Max.

"Yes," said the Oracle, "but especially people who are forward-thinking enough take advantage of the Wheel's potential. So when you say 'people,' bear in mind you're not talking about average folks."

"You know, maybe we are talking about *business* people," said Minnie. "Maybe they're more likely to be the first buyers."

"Excellent," said the Oracle. "Your first buyers—indeed, the first buyers of any truly new technology—are very likely to be people of means who can envision the Wheel as a way to make themselves more successful, to make their businesses more successful, to do things that have never been done before, to make life *better*."

"I get the sense you're talking about a fairly small number of people here," said Max.

"Yes, I am," said the Oracle. "In the early going, all new technology begins with a very small base of customers who have surplus wealth to risk on it. But a small customer base, for you, is not such a bad thing. Because when you're first starting out, you don't have the resources to sell this to the whole world. You have to focus your attentions on only the best prospects."

"Yes," said Max, "but *who* might those prospects be? *Specifically?* Do you know anybody?"

"Sorry, we who deal in the oracular don't divulge specifics. It's against our code. That's for you two to figure out."

Max and Minnie looked askance at him.

"However," said the Oracle, "by answering the bedrock questions, you know pretty well who your first customers are *likely* to be. And you know who your competitors are. Now, my bedrock question number four: Why are those first customers going to buy from *you*?"

"From us?" asked Minnie. "They have no choice. We are the only ones who make the Wheel."

"*But* they do have a choice. You do have competitors. Which takes us to bedrock question number five: Why might they prefer to continue buying from your competitors—and not from *you*?"

"I don't know," said Minnie. "Because they're dolts?"

"Right, because they're locked into the past," said Max. "Because they have no vision."

"Arrogant," said the Oracle. "Very arrogant on your part—but also very typical of inventors, entrepreneurs, and anyone with new ideas. Actually, there are good reasons why potential customers would keep on buying elephants and sledges from your competition."

"Why is that?" asked Minnie.

"Your competitors offer proven, reliable, affordable, low-tech methods that are well understood and don't require vision. Even a complete dolt can use them. And there are a lot of dolts in this world. That's why you should not underestimate your competition's strength."

Somewhat insulted, Max said to Minnie, "Well, I think I've heard enough."

At that moment the Oracle was covering a yawn with the palm of his hand. "Good," he said. "It's time for my power nap."

"But wait," said Minnie. "Can't you tell us more?"

"What do you expect for a skewer of roasted goat?" The old man got up to leave but, seeing the expression on Minnie's face, he relented. "All right, I'll give you the sixth bedrock question: Given everything we've just talked about, what *added values* do your salespeople have to supply in order for customers to buy from you rather than from your competitors?"

In unison, Max and Minnie shrugged.

"That's it," said the Oracle. "You're on your own. Nice meeting both of you. Good luck with the Wheel."

And with that, the Oracle faded back into the nether reaches of the gloomy cave.

Minnie's Notes . . .

Ozzie the Oracle's 6 Bedrock Questions

1. Who are our customers?

2. Who are our competitors?

3. Why do customers want what we are selling?

4. What would make them prefer to buy from us?

5. Why might they prefer to buy from our competitors?

6. What added values does our salesperson have to offer to make a sale?

Max and Minnie packed up and went back down the mountain. They returned the way they had come, through the bugs and snakes, through the long winding canyon, along the river, and into town.

Wiping the sweat from his forehead as he went through the door when they got home, Max began to vent. "What a waste of time that was!"

"Oh, now, now," said Minnie. "He might not have given us many clear answers, but he did give us some great questions."

Max rumbled and grumbled into the kitchen to get himself some cool refreshment.

"Listen," said his wife, "why don't we just sit down and go over those questions again, just to see where we stand?"

So they did.

After a while, they had written out the answers to five out of the six bedrock questions.

Minnie's Notes . . .

Bedrock Question #1:
Who are our customers?
- Those who need to move big, heavy stuff faster, easier, and cheaper.

Bedrock Question #2:
Who are our competitors?
- Everyone who sells established methods of moving heavy loads (for example, elephant and camel dealers, sledge makers).

Bedrock Question #3:
Why do customers want what we are selling?
- They're looking for the big performance gain promised by new technology.
- The Wheel offers the opportunity to do things that could not be done before.

Bedrock Question #4:
What would make them prefer to buy from us?
- We are the Wheel's only provider.

Bedrock Question #5:
Why might they prefer to buy from our competitors?
- Competitors offer proven, affordable methods.
- Customers don't understand our technology.

Bedrock Question #6:
What added values does our salesperson have to offer to make a sale?
- ????????

"If we could just answer that sixth question," said Minnie, "maybe we could really figure this out."

"Why? I don't see what's so important about that," said Max. "I just want to know who's going to buy my Wheels."

"Well . . . who needs to move lots of heavy things faster, easier, and cheaper than they do now?"

Max thought a moment. "What about farmers? They always have to move dirt and produce and that kind of thing."

"True. But the farmers around here don't have much money. What about selling your Wheels to caravans? Moving lots of stuff is their whole business."

Max nodded. "It's a possibility . . . but caravans have to go over mountains and across deserts. Wheels work best on roads and hard, level ground."

"Okay, then . . . what about builders? What about the construction business?"

At this, Max's eyes widened. "That's it! Why didn't I think of this before?"

He jumped to his feet.

"Minnie, I am going back to Egypt."

"Egypt? But, Max, that's such a long trip. Why do you want to go there?"

"Because that's where they're building the Pyramid. That's where I'm going to sell my Wheels. I'll sell them all to the Pyramid builders and make a fortune!"

Early the next morning, Max packed his Wheels and Axles onto some donkeys and set off for Egypt.

Weeks later, he arrived at the construction site of the first Pyramid. Surveying the scene, Max saw thousands of sweaty bodies laboring in the sun. He saw lots of big cut stones waiting to be moved. Dozens of expensive elephants were slowly dragging the heaviest of loads. And off in the distance was the Pyramid itself, which was actually starting to *look* like a pyramid after so many years of work.

"This is it," said Max. "These people are my customers. And they are going to make me a wealthy man when I ease their burdens."

Max set to it. He went right up to a group of workers struggling to move a huge, heavy stone and said, "Excuse me, but I've got something that would make your jobs a heck of a lot easier. It's called the Wheel. And if you will give me a few minutes of your time, I will demonstrate how it works."

The workers naturally were more than happy to take a break, and after persuading several of the quarry workers to assist him, Max assembled two sets of Wheels and Axles, and with a big heave-ho was able to get the humongous stone loaded onto this strange new device. After lashing the stone to the Axles so it wouldn't fall off, Max proceeded to show the Pyramid workers how easy it was to move something big and heavy with the aid of this new technology. After rolling the huge stone back and forth a few times, several of the workers even applauded. It was like a miracle!

"So, how many Wheels would you guys like?"

"We'd like a bunch of them," said one of the workers.

"Great!" said Max. "It's only a thousand shekels a Wheel and five hundred per Axle—and I'll be happy to accept a check."

"Well, ah, that's the problem," said the worker. "We don't have any money."

"Yeah," said another. "I mean, if it was up to us, and we had the money, we'd buy your Wheels. But it's not up to us, and we can't afford them."

Just then the Pyramid workers' supervisor came by.

"Hey! Let's move those stones!" he yelled. "And you!" he called to Max. "What are you doing here?"

"Um . . . Hi! My name is Max, and I have this terrific labor-saving device called a Wheel. Allow me to demonstrate—"

"Get that stone down off that . . . that . . . whatever it is, *get the stone off of it!*"

"But you don't understand," said Max.

"No, I don't," said the supervisor. "They don't pay me to understand, they pay me to keep these guys moving the stones!"

Befuddled and frustrated, Max put his Wheels and Axles back

on the donkeys and wandered about the construction site looking for someone with the authority to make a buying decision.

Eventually, after asking about, Max found himself in front of a large tent with a sign in front of it that read PYRAMID PURCHASING AGENT.

Following a long wait, Max was shown in to see the top purchasing agent for the Pyramid project, Mr. Granite.

Well, Mr. Granite had neither the time nor the interest in a demonstration of the Wheel. Indeed, he was rather annoyed at this guy who had shown up without an appointment and was delivering this spiel about *rolling* things from place to place rather than dragging them.

"Wait a minute," Mr. Granite interrupted. "What in the world are you talking about? We've got thousands of big, sweaty guys with strong backs to do our stone hauling."

"Yes, but what about the really huge and heavy stones? My Wheel technology will do it better and faster!"

Mr. Granite shrugged. "We use elephants."

"Excuse me?"

"When we need to move the truly humongous stones, we use elephants."

"But don't you see? The Wheel can save you lots of money *and* get the job done quicker!"

"Look," said Mr. Granite, "our good Pharaoh has on the payroll the smartest and most technically advanced engineers and architects anywhere in the known world. If this Wheel thing were really worth anything, they'd have come up with it themselves—and they'd have given me a specification to buy it from somebody."

Exasperated, Max sputtered, "But, but . . ."

"Pardon me, but I do have an important meeting scheduled with my chisel vendor."

"Mr. Granite, please! The Wheel is the wave of the future—"

"Sir, we don't have time for that wave-of-the-future stuff. We've got a Pyramid to build."

* * *

Back home again in Sumeria, Max told his wife his sad story.

"It was just what the Oracle predicted," said Max. "Our competition is the established technology. The conventional ways of doing things. And the people who might be our customers don't want to change! Here I thought all I had to do was just show them the Wheel and they'd line up to buy. I had no idea it would be this hard."

"But there has to be a way," said Minnie. For by now, these were not just Max's Wheels, but hers as well.

Max stood up and paced. "You know what the big problem is? It's me. I am just not a salesman. A real salesperson could have sold the Wheel. Would have found the right people to talk to. Would have said the magic words that would have made the sale. But that's not me. Never will be."

Minnie thought about this and said, "Then why don't you hire someone to sell your Wheels for you? You know, someone with experience. A *sales professional*."

Max considered this. "Yeah, but what are we going to use to pay this person? I spent all my spare cash on that trip to Egypt. All I've got left is tied up in Wheels!"

His wife, however, already had an answer. "Let's talk to my parents. They have money. Maybe they'll lend us some to get the business started."

The following evening, Minnie invited her folks for dinner, and after a delicious meal of figs and a camel fricassee, Max proceeded to demonstrate the Wheel to his in-laws. Within a few hours it was settled: Minnie's parents would finance the start-up of the Wheel business, but only under one condition.

"And what's that?" asked Max.

"We want Minnie to handle the marketing," said her parents.

Now, you might find this hard to believe, but in the olden

days, people were not as enlightened as we are now. Back then, women almost always did the marketing.

"All right," said Max. "No problem. It's a deal."

So, the next day, Minnie's parents went to the bank and got the money to get the Wheel business started.

Right away, Minnie posted an advertisement in the town square: SALESPERSON WANTED: MUST HAVE EXPERIENCE.

The next morning, lined up at the front door were three people ready to apply for the job. Minnie collected their résumés, then invited the man at the front of the line inside.

"Hi, I'm Caleb," he said. "They call me the Captain of Sales."

"The Captain of Sales? My, that sounds very impressive. Tell me, have you been in sales very long?"

"Years. I've sold everything from camels to kumquats."

"That's quite a range. But, excuse me for putting it bluntly . . . how do I know you're really good?"

"Well, in my last job, I won three awards for delivering great customer service."

"Really? That settles it. How would you like to start selling Wheels?"

"Um . . . terrific! But . . . it might help if you first tell me what a Wheel *is*."

"Let me show you," said Minnie.

After she put one of her husband's Wheels through its paces, the Captain of Sales said, "I think I should have no problem selling this. I know exactly what to do."

"You're sure?"

"Absolutely. Just leave everything to me."

So Minnie hired the Captain and sent the other applicants away.

Months later, Max went to Minnie and asked, "When is this Captain of Sales going to launch our product?"

"Well, I've been keeping it a surprise, because the Captain needed time to get things set up. But next Monday is the Grand Opening."

"The Grand Opening?"

"Of the New, Super Wheel Store!"

Sure enough, when Monday arrived, Minnie took Max into town, and there, on the corner of Main and Hammurabi Streets, in a fashionable new upscale mini-mall near the amphitheater, was a huge store with a great big sign: MAX'S WHEELS.

In the windows were colorful banners proclaiming "Low, low prices!" and "E-Z Credit!" and "We deliver!"

Inside, all the Wheels were on display. Young, fresh-faced clerks bounded over, eager to be of service, as soon as Max and Minnie entered.

"Thanks, but we're the owners," Max explained.

"Oh," one of the young clerks said. "We were hoping you'd be a customer. There haven't been many people coming in all day."

"But I'm sure things will pick up very soon," said the Captain of Sales, stepping from behind the counter. "We've got people going from neighborhood to neighborhood broadcasting news of our special sale and handing out our special coupons."

"Coupons?" asked Max. "Are you sure this is the right approach?"

"It worked in my last job."

"And what was that?"

"Selling kumquats—as well as dates, oranges, and lemons."

"Lemons. You sold . . . fruit?"

"I didn't just sell fruit, Max. I sold *lots* of fruit. And I'm telling you, if you want to sell Wheels, this is the way to do it: a big store in a convenient location. Lots of inventory. Low prices. Ready credit. And a courteous, energetic staff offering great customer service."

A month later, the Captain wasn't quite so confident.

"I'm sorry, but I don't know what went wrong. Everything I've done here in this store worked wonderfully with fruit—and camels, too!"

"Well," said Max, "could it be that selling fruit and camels is not the same thing as selling Wheels? I mean, everybody knows what to do with fruit. And everybody these days knows how to ride a camel. But nobody knows how to use a Wheel because they've just been invented! Hardly anybody has even heard of a Wheel. Why would customers take time to come into a store that's selling something they don't even know what to do with? Shouldn't you get out there and knock on some doors or something? Shouldn't you show people what the product is?"

Red-faced, the Captain just stared at the floor.

"Okay, just tell me this," said Max. "Exactly how many Wheels have you sold?"

"One," said the Captain.

"One?"

"Actually . . . none."

"None," muttered Max.

"You see, we did sell one Wheel—and we delivered it promptly, the same day, in fact. But the customer brought it back a week later. Said it didn't match her carpet."

"Her carpet? Why did that matter?"

"She wanted to use it as a coffee table. Anyway, under the terms of our 30-Day, One Hundred Percent-Satisfaction Guarantee, we cheerfully accepted the return and credited a refund. Other than that . . ."

Max turned to Minnie and shook his head.

"Captain, I hate to say this," said Minnie, "but we're running out of money. We're going to have to let you go."

So Max and Minnie closed the Super Wheel Store. They gave the Captain of Sales and his cheerful young sales associates their pay. They removed the Wheel inventory. Then Max looked at his wife and said, "You're still in charge of marketing. What do we do now?"

Minnie sighed. "Well, we still have some money from my parents left. And we still have the résumés of those other two salespeople who answered the ad. Why don't we see if one of those two can help us?"

They read the résumés, and as it turned out, only one of the two had any real experience selling. So they chose that person, gave him a call, and the next day, the applicant came to see them.

"Hello, you must be Max and Minnie," said the man, extending his hand. "I'm Ben the Builder."

"Why do they call you 'the Builder'?" asked Minnie.

"Because I build solid sales year after year. I'm steady, dependable. I'm loyal to my customers, and they are loyal to me."

"Well, that sounds like what we need," said Minnie.

"All right, here's the situation," said her husband. "We have a brand-new product that we think has lots of promise. But we need someone to get out there and show it to customers and bring back some sales."

"No problem," said Ben. "I have terrific, long-term relationships with a number of well-heeled, respectable customers. I can call on these people, show them the Wheel, and make a number of suggestions as to how it might best suit their needs."

"Excellent!" said Max.

"You're just the kind of person we need," said Minnie. "The only trouble is, we're a little short of cash right now, and I don't know if the salary we have to offer will be adequate for someone with your contacts and experience."

They talked it over, and Ben the Builder at last held up his hand, saying "Don't worry. Tell you what. I'll take the salary you can pay me, and whenever I do sell a Wheel, you can pay me a commission. That way, the added cost to you will be covered by the income from the sale."

"All right," said Minnie. "You're hired."

But a month or so later, Ben was back.

"I hate to admit it," he said, "but I think I might have made a mistake. Things just aren't going the way I thought they would."

"Why is that?" asked Minnie.

"Well, every morning since I first met with you, I've been getting up early, going out, and calling on my customers. I've shown them the Wheel, and I've talked it up. I've told them how great it is. But nobody's interested in buying one."

"Nobody?" asked Max.

"Now, you should understand these are my regular customers,

and we've been dealing with each other for a long time. I've always been straight with them, and most of the time, they've always been straight with me. Everybody thinks the Wheel is cool. But they're not sure what to do with it."

"What do you mean, they're not sure what to do with it?" Max asked. "Didn't you show them? They can use it to move things!"

"Yeah, I showed them," said Ben. "And they all got the point. But using a Wheel to move stuff just isn't what they're used to. When my customers want to move heavy loads, they use camels and horses and elephants and—"

"Big sweaty guys with strong backs," Max finished.

"Exactly. Now, let me make a suggestion. If your company had horses or elephants to sell, I know my customers would buy them. I know I could make that kind of a sale. Or let's take your big sweaty guys with strong backs—suppose you two started a temporary employment services company. I could sell the service contracts and you two could handle recruiting and payroll and the rest of the business end. What do you think?"

"No, I'm sorry," said Max. "That's not what we're about."

Ben the Builder sighed deeply, then shrugged his shoulders. "Well, believe me, I gave it my best shot. Listen, I'm on your side. I think the Wheel has a lot of potential and it could be a great product someday. Right now, though, the Wheel is ahead of its time—at least for my customers it is."

So, with regret, Ben the Builder resigned.

"Well, who's left?" Max asked.

Minnie produced the last résumé. "Her name is Toby. She's just out of college. She's got a master's degree in . . . I don't know, something technical. And she's a certified, licensed wizard."

"All right, what the heck," said Max. "Let's talk to her."

When they got together with Toby the Wizard, they found her to be a pleasant but assertive young woman—a bit geeky, but quite professional in appearance and demeanor. And obviously she was very smart. Right off the bat, she understood the value of the Wheel and how important it could someday become, and within minutes she was asking Max intelligent questions about the new technology.

"The only problem, as I see it," said Minnie, "is that you don't have any actual experience in sales."

"That's true," said Toby, "but I'm what's known as a 'quick study.' I'll stop at the bookstore on my way home and pick up a couple of books on selling. I'm not a born salesperson—my long-term goal, if you want to know the truth, is to be in management—but I'll figure it out. With some basic skills and some practice, I think I can get the job done."

"Okay," said Max, "but what are you going to do about finding customers?"

"When I was doing research at the university, I made some contacts in the business world," she said. "I'll start with those and see where they lead."

Max and Minnie both looked at each other and said, "Why not?"

"Great," said the young woman. "I'm truly excited about going to work for you. This could be a terrific growth company."

"Well, if you can bring in the sales," said Minnie, "you're going to have a bright future with us."

Yet another month went by. Then one day, Toby came by to report what she thought was good news.

"I think I might have a sale," she said.

"Really?" said Minnie.

"Yes, and it's a project that could show the world what the Wheel can do."

"Wow, that's great," said Max. "But you say this is a . . . project?"

"Right. I have a potential client who's interested, but we're going to have to adapt the Wheel to their needs. My thought was to combine the Wheel with some other components I have in mind and create a system—"

"Now, wait a minute," said Max. "How long is all of this going to take?"

"I'd say six to nine months tops."

"For the whole project?"

"No, to bring in the sale. See, we'll have to do some design and testing work on our end to convince them that this is going to be worthwhile. Then we'll probably go to a pilot project that will run for a year or so. And then, based on that, they might want to roll it out—"

"Hold it, hold it," said Max. "You don't seem to get it. We've got tons of Wheels that are already made. They're ready to go, and we need someone to sell them *now*—not six months or a year down the road."

"Toby, I'm sorry. I know you were excited and that you really threw yourself into it," said Minnie, "but we're out of money. We just can't afford the kind of time you're talking about."

And with that, Toby the Wizard went the way of the other two salespeople.

6

"That's it; the story's over," said Max. "We spent all the money. We didn't make any sales. We're out of business."

"Yes, but what are we going to do about this mess?" asked Minnie.

"I don't know how we'll ever pay back your parents. We'll have to go explain it to them."

"No, I mean this mess of Wheels. How are we going to get rid of them?"

Max sadly shook his head. "Well, as you once suggested, I guess we'll just have to roll them into the river."

"Wait," said Minnie. "Before we do that, why don't we go talk to the Oracle one more time?"

"I don't see what good it will do," said her husband, "but, hey, one more trek into the wilderness can't do us any harm, can it?"

So, once again, Max and Minnie left the city and followed the path along the river, up through the winding canyon, and into the hot desert mountains where nothing grew except the afore-mentioned bugs and snakes.

When they finally arrived at the cave, Max built a fire and Minnie prepared the offering that they had brought with them. Soon, the smell of food drifted back into the dark, dank reaches—and presto, the Oracle appeared.

"You again?" said the old man. Then he sniffed the aromas coming from the fire. "Mmmm . . . what *is* that?"

"Camel kabobs," said Minnie. "Here, try one."

The Oracle plucked a hot skewer out of the fire, blew on it, and then bit in. "Not bad."

"They're marinated," said Minnie.

"Well . . . a bit chewy, but otherwise, I must admit, quite delicious."

"And we thought you might like a side dish. Here, have some hummus and fresh pita bread."

The Oracle sampled some, then nodded approvingly, sat down on a rock, and polished off the whole meal.

Sated at last, he patted his stomach and said, "Okay, what's your problem now?"

"Our problem is we still can't sell any Wheels," said Max.

"Why am I not surprised?"

"But you see," said Minnie, "we even went to the expense of hiring three different salespeople."

"Three? What kind of salespeople were they?"

"*Bad* salespeople, if you ask me," said Max.

He and Minnie gave the old man a complete rundown on what had happened.

When they finished, the Oracle said, "Listen, these were *not* bad salespeople. The problem is that they were bad for your particular situation. See, centuries ago, way back at the dawn of the sales profession, someone foisted upon us the myth of the universal 'good' salesperson—someone who can sell any product to anyone at any time, any place, and can do it consistently, time and again.

"Now, I can't tell you that such a beast doesn't exist. But I can tell you that I've never met one. And I do believe that unicorns are more plentiful. The reality is that there are different kinds of good salespeople, and the kind you need right now isn't any of those three you tried."

"Well, what kind of salesperson do we need?" asked Minnie.

"You need to find yourselves a closer."

"A closer? What's a closer?"

"Closers," said the Oracle, "are a special and rather rare breed of salesperson. Most salespeople sell a solution to a problem. Closers, however, are in a league of their own. Closers sell dreams. They sell a better tomorrow. They sell opportunity."

"Yeah, but we want to sell Wheels," said Max.

"And Wheels are the future. You still do believe that, don't you?"

"Yes, I do."

"Ah, but neither you nor you wife—nor any of the salespeople you tried—can spin the special magic it takes to get someone else to believe in that future."

"True."

"That's why you need a closer," said the Oracle. "Because a closer will join the crusade—if it's lucrative enough—and will find those first customers and get them to believe and be a part of the better tomorrow you want to create by way of this new technology called the Wheel."

"All right, then, how do we find a closer?" asked Minnie.

"That is often the hard part. Closers are rare individuals. Lots of salespeople can be trained to close a sale. But the true closer is *born* to close. Closers believe totally in what they're selling, and they live for that golden moment of getting a brand-new customer to say yes. They have a quality of drive, determination, and focus that you won't find in more than one in a hundred salespeople."

"But where would we start to look?"

"Often as not, it's the closer who finds you," said the Oracle.

"How would we even recognize one?"

"Look at what this person has been selling and how he or she has been selling it. Closers tend toward high-end new technology that is revolutionary and has no imitators. They also gravitate to products that are unique and exclusive. Closers have a very high energy level. They have an aura of success about them. They communicate the image of that success in what they wear, what they buy, where they live. But the best way to recognize true closers is to watch them work."

"How's that?"

"Closers can sell an expensive product or service right now, today, to people who have never heard of that product or service until the closer knocked on their door. And the closers and their customers often enough are strangers—have never met before, and may never meet again."

"Wow. That *is* someone special," said Minnie.

"The trouble is," said Max, "even if we find a closer, we're out of money. We can't pay anything up front, not until we've actually sold some Wheels."

"This is one case when you might be in luck," said the Oracle. "Because closers usually don't work for a salary. They work on straight commission and get a percentage of every sale."

"How much?"

"Oh, ten, fifteen, maybe even fifty percent."

"Fifty percent?"

"Sometimes higher," said the Oracle. "It depends. It's whatever the closer can negotiate. So if you do find one, be careful what you sign away."

"Okay, but do you know any closers? Can you give us any names?"

The Oracle thought for a moment. "Yes, I do know of one. Let me see if I still have his card."

He searched the many pockets inside his robe and finally produced a business card that he handed to Minnie.

CASSIUS THE CLOSER
President
CASSIUS SALES ENTERPRISES

bmahr Y ¿vxtsg

"You might try him—though whether he will help you or not is . . . well, who can say?"

"Is he any good?" asked Minnie.

"Any good?" retorted the Oracle. "Who do you think sold me this cave?"

So it came to pass that Max and Minnie sought out this guy named Cassius.

With some Wheels and Axles loaded on donkeys, they made the journey to his office, but when they arrived, the receptionist informed them that Cassius was out and that he might not even return that day.

"It's very important that we speak to him, if only for a few minutes," said Minnie. "Can you maybe tell us where we might look for him?"

"I know he has an appointment later today over on Sun God Avenue," said the receptionist. "You might be able to catch him there."

Max and Minnie went to the address the receptionist wrote down for them. There, they found themselves in a very well-to-do neighborhood with palaces lining the street. But they discovered a small park with a bench in the shade of a date palm, and so they tied the donkeys to the palm and sat down to wait.

Before very long, up the street came a young man wearing a turban on his head and riding a camel. He parked the camel in the street, dismounted, and untied a rolled-up carpet from the hump of the camel.

Minnie's Notes . . .

Closers often start their own companies—or otherwise work for themselves. Few work as employees, especially not for large corporations, where their values would clash with those of the organization.

Then he took the carpet across the street and knocked on the front door of a palace.

"Do you think that's him?" asked Minnie.

"Nah! Too young. He's just a used-rug salesman," said Max.

But as they watched, the owner of the palace appeared. After a few words, the man with the carpet unfurled it on the front lawn.

"Look, what did I tell you?" Max said to Minnie. "A palace like that, the guy's got to have all the rugs he could ever want. Lotsa luck selling him another one."

Shortly, however, the young man in the turban and the rich guy both stepped onto the carpet. They sat down. The man in the turban clapped his hands, and—to Max's and Minnie's utter astonishment—the carpet rose into the air. He clapped his hands again and *zoom!*—off they went. They flew down the street, banked left, flew between a couple of houses, banked right, did a loop-de-loop and then a barrel roll, and then the carpet landed right back on the lawn of the rich guy's palace.

> **Minnie's Notes . . .**
>
> A hallmark of the closer is the ability to complete the sales transaction in one or two contacts with the customer.

The two talked. Max and Minnie could hear only a few words every now and then, but it seemed the rich guy was definitely interested in the carpet, though he appeared to be weighing the decision. He kept stroking his chin. He would lean one way, then the other, as the man in the turban proceeded to do most of the talking, gestured excitedly, and at one point counted on his fingers what seemed to be the many reasons why the other man needed this flying carpet.

Finally, the man in the turban looked up at the angle of the sun and said it was time to go, that he had another appointment.

"No, no, wait!" the rich guy all but shouted. "I'll take it."

He disappeared into his mansion, but came back a few minutes later bearing five or six bags of gold. These he gave to the man in the turban. They shook hands. Then the rich guy clapped his hands and flew off to show his new possession to all his friends—and, who knows, maybe even his rivals.

The young man in the turban hefted the bags of money and began to walk back to his camel, at which point Minnie said to Max, "That's him! I just know it is!"

Minnie's Notes . . .

A closer's classic tactic to make the sale: withdraw the offer.

By now, the man was tying the bags of gold to the camel's saddle, and Minnie approached him.

"Excuse me," she said, "but is your name Cassius by any chance?"

"Yes, it is. I'm Cassius the Closer."

"My name is Minnie, and this his my husband, Max. We couldn't help but notice—"

"The flying carpet? Yes, a truly amazing new technology. You know, with a flying carpet, you can zip straight to Damascus in an hour and change."

"That's very impressive, but—"

"Impressive? Think of it! Can you just imagine the impact on society? Why, it's going to revolutionize personal transportation! And the lucky few able to buy them now are going to have something that will be the envy of their peers."

Minnie's Notes . . .

Closers like Cassius are drawn toward selling exotic, high-tech, high-margin products—but only those that entail a simple sales transaction, requiring no extended relationship with the customer.

"Well, I'd love to try one—"

"Would you? Well, I would love to demonstrate one for you. Tell me, which of these magnificent mansions is yours?"

"Oh, we don't live around here."

"I see," said Cassius. "Well, unfortunately, I must be on my way. That flying carpet I just sold was my last. Now I have to wait for my agents in Persia to replenish my supply."

"Actually," said Max, "what really impressed us wasn't the flying carpet but the way you sold it. I mean, you just came right in, got the guy's attention, took him for a ride, and you got the sale. You must be one heck of a salesman."

Cassius modestly shrugged. "Well, thank you. Of course, I should be pretty good at selling by now. I've been doing it for twenty years."

Max looked closely at Cassius. "You've been a salesman for twenty years? But you can't be a day over thirty years old!"

"Yes, but I started when I was ten," said Cassius. "Not flying carpets, mind you. Selling pottery door-to-door, that kind of thing."

> ### Minnie's Notes . . .
>
> Closers are naturally drawn to sales, and often gain their first selling experiences when they are teenagers or even younger.

"You seem very successful," said Minnie, eyeing the ruby on his turban.

Cassius leaned close to them and said in a confidential tone, "I'll tell you, I could retire right now if I wanted to and live a life of leisure and luxury just from what I've earned over the past few years."

"Really? Then why don't you, may I ask?"

"Because I believe in flying carpets," Cassius said with conviction. "And I believe that when I sell that flying carpet technology to the world, the world will be a better place. It's a passion with me. It's what gets me out of bed in the morning and keeps me going until late at night. Someday

> ### Minnie's Notes . . .
>
> Closers are motivated by a passion for what they are selling, but also by the notion that you can't have too much money.

flying carpets will fill the skies—and I will have been the one who made that possible. And on that day," he added with a smile, "I'm going to be the richest dude on the planet!"

And as Max and Minnie listened, there was not the tiniest doubt in their minds that Cassius truly meant what he said.

With a small wave to them, Cassius said good-bye and began to get on his camel.

"Wait!" said Minnie. "Cassius, please don't go yet."

"Why? What's the matter?"

"You see," she said, "my husband here is an inventor, and he has developed a revolutionary new product."

"It's true," said Max. "As a matter of fact, this thing that I have invented might just have even more impact on the world than the flying carpet."

Skeptical, Cassius said, "Really? And what exactly is this 'new' product you've come up with?"

"We happen to have some samples right here," Max said with a gesture. "We call it the Wheel."

An hour later, Max and Minnie had struck a deal with Cassius the Closer. It was agreed that Cassius, rather than waiting months or years for more flying carpets to arrive from Persia, would instead sell the Wheel. He would not be paid a salary, but would instead work entirely on commission. And the commission was sizable: For every Wheel he sold, Cassius would keep fifty percent of the selling price.

They scribbled out a contract on the spot, and everybody signed. As soon as the ink was dry, Cassius took two sets of Wheels and Axles to use as samples. Then, to Max's and Minnie's surprise, he took the saddle off his camel and removed the saddle blanket.

The saddle blanket was not what it appeared to be. It was a light, strong piece of very thin carpet folded many times—and Cassius now unfolded it. And unfolded it. And unfolded it, until it was as large as the carpet he had just sold. Cassius spoke a few magic words, clapped his hands—and the blanket became as stiff as a board and rose into the air, hovering just slightly off the ground.

"Hey, I thought you said that flying carpet you just sold was your last one," said Max.

"I always keep a spare for myself, just in case of . . . well, you know, emergencies," Cassius said with a wink.

Max and Minnie exchanged a glance. But Cassius nonchalantly loaded his things and the Wheels and Axles onto his special carpet. He then settled himself in the middle and said to them, "Well, I'm off."

"What about your camel?" asked Minnie.

"Too slow for the distance I'll be traveling. You can have her. In a few days, I'll have earned enough to buy a thousand camels."

His confidence made the couple smile. The three shook hands, then Cassius the Closer clapped his hands again. The carpet rose, and with a wave, the salesman zoomed off into the bright, blue sky.

Max and Minnie, each holding a rein of the camel, watched until Cassius had vanished over the horizon.

"I guess he's what you call a high flyer," said Max.

"Yes, well, I just hope we did the right thing. A fifty percent commission on every sale seems awfully high."

"Minnie, we weren't making any money anyway, so what difference does it make? Fifty percent of something is better than a hundred percent of zero."

The two of them took the camel and the donkeys and headed for home. Meanwhile, cruising in a cloudless sky, Cassius the Closer scanned the landscape below, looking for signs that might suggest the location of the world's first buyer of the Wheel.

7

Before sunset that day, Cassius was circling over the construction site of the first Pyramid. He observed the thousands of workers and hundreds of elephants and all the tens of thousands of stones lying about, waiting to be placed in the monument. But Cassius didn't land.

Instead, he continued to circle in wider and wider arcs around the site until he was a considerable distance away from the Pyramid—several days' travel by foot. Eventually, he saw a rather large hole in the ground. Upon flying closer, he detected that it was what he'd first thought: a stone quarry.

"This looks good," he said to himself.

He then flew to the nearest town, spent the night at the local inn, and got up early the next morning to begin making his preparations.

When all was ready, Cassius got onto his carpet. He flew to the stone quarry and landed right in the middle of it, making quite an impression upon all who saw him.

"Where would I find the owner of this quarry?" he asked the throng of workers who had gathered around him.

"Do you have an appointment?" asked a man who was dressed better than most of the workers and was apparently in a position of some authority.

"I have to speak to the owner about a very important matter that concerns the Pharaoh," said Cassius.

"Oh. Well, ah . . . right this way."

The man escorted Cassius to a plain, not very impressive building at the edge of the quarry. There was a brief delay before a barrel-chested, bald man emerged from some offices in the rear of the building.

"I'm Mr. Marble, the quarry owner. What can I do for you?"

"Pleased to meet you. I'm Cassius the Closer. Is there someplace private where we can talk?"

Mr. Marble took Cassius into his office. After offering honey cakes and fresh coffee, Mr. Marble asked, "You have some kind of news for me about the Pharaoh?"

"I have an important matter to discuss with you that concerns the Pharaoh and the Pyramid he's building. But first, tell me please, what kind of stone do you cut in this quarry?"

"In this particular quarry, we cut limestone, but I have several others.

Minnie's Notes . . .

The closer doesn't bother trying to sell to subordinates like purchasing agents. They don't have the authority to approve radical new technologies. So the closer seeks out and sells to the top decision maker.

Minnie's Notes . . .

The best closers are ethical, but they are also highly manipulative—in fact, they must be to do what they do.

Our company offers granite, sandstone, and my family's own special marble as well."

"And it's of fine quality?"

"The best!"

"Yet you don't currently supply any stone for the Pharaoh's Pyramid?" asked Cassius, making a calculated guess.

"No, I'm afraid not," said Mr. Marble. "Wish that we could, but the logistics of delivering the stone . . .we're just too far away from the construction site for it to be practical. Believe me, I'd love to have even a piece of that contract. Every year, we submit our bid, but the expense of hiring all those people to drag the stone to the site . . . hell, even if we brought in elephants, there's just no way we could get our price competitive and still make a profit."

Cassius leaned forward. "Mr. Marble, I have the power to change that for you. More exactly, I can give you the power to deliver your stone to the Pyramid—or anywhere else—more quickly and more economically than was ever thought possible."

Mr. Marble chuckled. "What, with that flying gizmo that brought you here?"

"No. As marvelous as my flying carpet is, it wouldn't get off the ground with stones the size of those you need to move. But I do happen to be the sole representative throughout the world of a new technology—revolutionary, yet simple and practical—that can move your stones with an efficiency that until now you could only dream of."

"Yeah? What is it?"

"I have to show it to you, Mr. Marble. You have to see it to believe it." Cassius stood up and gestured toward the door. "Right this way."

As they were about to leave the building, Cassius turned and said to the quarry owner, "Oh, by the way, do you have a cloak or something to wrap around you? Even though we're in the Sahara Desert, at the speeds and altitudes we'll be traveling, it can get a little chilly up there."

"Oh . . . you mean we'll be flying?"

"I'll have you back within the hour."

"Well, ah . . . I did have some staff meetings scheduled."

"Mr. Marble, what I'm about to show you could—and I'm actually being maybe a little conservative when I say this—could triple or quadruple the revenue and profitability of your quarry business within a matter of just a few years. It will give you a realistic chance at winning the Pyramid stone contract—and that's just the beginning."

Mr. Marble nodded slowly, then grabbed the cloak he sometimes wore at night for the cool desert air, and began walking toward Cassius the Closer's flying carpet.

> ### Minnie's Notes . . .
>
> The first buyers of a new technology are often called gate swingers—for being the first through the gate. Though small in number, they are the prime market for closers, whose challenge it is to find them.

Now, bear in mind that a closer of the modern era would use private aircraft and limousines and such to accomplish what Cassius did with his flying carpet. But the effect was the same. In a few minutes, they were airborne, and Mr. Marble was smiling and having a good time.

"Hey, this is fun!" he said.

"I have more of these on order—each one is hand-made, of course—and next time I have one available I'll fly in to have you try it out."

"Great!"

Just for entertainment, Cassius performed a few aggressive flying maneuvers, then brought the carpet in for a gentle landing outside the town where he had spent the night.

Waiting in readiness were a number of townspeople whom Cassius had recruited and paid somewhat handsomely from the proceeds of his last flying carpet sale. They were assembled in two teams, each next to a humongous stone to be moved.

"Now, Mr. Marble, on the left we have Team A, which will move its stone by means of the attached ropes, dragging it across the ground. And on the right we have Team B, which will move its humongous stone by means of the revolutionary new technology of which I spoke: the Wheel."

"The Whe-e-e-l?"

"That's right, the Wheel. And if you look carefully, you'll see that Team B is actually at a considerable disadvantage to Team A because we have given them a much larger and heavier humongous stone to move," said Cassius. And at this, he cupped his hands and called, "Are you ready, Teams? Now, we all know the rules, don't we? The team to move its stone a distance of one hundred cubits across the finish line will win the prize of fifty shekels to be divided among its members! On your mark, get set . . . go!"

> **Minnie's Notes . . .**
>
> A closer's sales presentations often have a dramatic flair.

It was hardly even a race. Team B, which had its humongous stone mounted and securely lashed to the Axles between two sets of Wheels, pulled its load across the finish line well before Team A had dragged its stone even ten of the one hundred cubits.

"That's amazing!" said Mr. Marble. "I've never seen anything like it!"

"Until now, Mr. Marble, there never has been anything like it. Would you like to take a closer look?"

"Sure!"

They approached the big round Wheels, Mr. Marble said, "Well, they look sturdy enough."

"Sturdy? Go ahead and give 'em a kick if you don't think they're sturdy! This Wheel technology is revolutionary—yet simple, practical, and reliable. Here, take a look."

The two stooped down and peered beneath the big rock.

"You see, you've got your two Wheels attached to this crossbeam, called an Axle. Now, with lighter loads you can get away with one set of Wheels, but with big slabs of stone like this, you need sets, front and back. Then you get yourself some good, strong rope, and you tie one end of the rope to the Axle, wrap it few turns, put some turns around the load to secure it, then tie the rope down on the other side. Do that on both Axles—and you're on your way to the Pyramid!"

Mr. Marble smiled. "Well, as I told you, we don't have the stone contract for the Pyramid."

"Would you like to have it?"

"Yes."

"You can have it. You can get the Pyramid contract. And many others besides. With the Wheel,

> ## Minnie's Notes . . .
>
> ### The closer sells opportunity.

you have the competitive edge over every other stone quarry in Egypt. You can move your stones at least ten times faster than they can move theirs using the old, primitive dragging methods."

Marble, Cassius could see, was turning this over in his mind.

"And you know what's coming, don't you?" asked Cassius.

"What's coming?"

"It's the talk up and down the Nile! You can read the hieroglyphs on the wall! This Pyramid the Pharaoh is building is only the beginning. There will be other pyramids. Not to mention temples, and obelisks, and all kinds of other monuments. The military is talking about stone walls for cities! Stone, as a building material, is in its infancy! The future is incredible! And with Wheel technology to move it to where it's needed, it's going to be the stone from your quarries!"

Mr. Marble was staring off into the distance. He could see it all happening. Yes, maybe it was possible.

"You know, I was flying over the Nile yesterday," said Cassius, "and I looked down at some fabulous palaces and mansions with their gardens and their date palms and fountains. Not long from now, one of those places could be yours, Mr. Marble."

"Mine? I might be well-off, but I'm not that well-off."

"Oh, maybe not now, but in a few years . . . ? After the Wheel has made possible the doubling, tripling, maybe even quadrupling of your revenue and profit? You'll be able to get out of this desert, live where it's lush and green. You can have servants. Marry your sons and daughters to the offspring of the wealthy and noble. With the stone contract for the Pharaoh's Pyramid, you'll be an important man, someone to know."

"But how will I manage my quarries from so far away?"

"Why, with your new flying carpet, it'll be an easy commute!"

After that, Mr. Marble was no longer standing on the hot, dusty dirt, baking in the sun in the middle of nowhere. He was enjoying fruit punch next to the fountain in his garden above the Nile. He was whizzing about on his flying carpet, keeping watch on his empire of quarries and observing from on high the many loads of stone rolling toward the great cities of Egypt on Wheels going around and around . . .

8

"He bought *how many* Wheels?" asked Max.

"Twenty sets of two, including the Axles, at five thousand shekels a set."

"That's one hundred thousand shekels!" said Minnie.

"How could you get him to pay that much?" Max asked.

Cassius the Closer shrugged. "It was easy. To him, the Wheel is the means to millions of shekels. To the life of his dreams. Compared to that, Wheels are a bargain. Now . . ."

He hefted a heavy wooden chest he'd brought in with him and set it on Minnie's kitchen table. When he opened it, the couple's eyes got as big as the golden coins they saw.

"He gave us a fifty percent down payment. This is your half, twenty-five thousand. I left with him the sample Wheels I'd brought and told him that you would ship the remaining sets to him by caravan, C.O.D. So if you'll handle that, I'll be on my way."

"But won't you stay for dinner?" asked Minnie.

"Thank you, but time is shekels. I flew over dozens of other little stone quarries on the way back, and after I've covered those,
I've got people like the stone masons, the monument contractors—I'm telling you, the market for Wheels is wide open! I'm so
glad we ran into each other!"

"I am, too," said Max. "But really, I'm just flabbergasted that
you're able to sell our Wheels when Minnie and I flopped every
time *we* tried to sell them. I'd love to know how you work. Would
it be possible for us to accompany you on a few of your trips?
We've still got plenty of Wheels in inventory, and I promise we
won't get in your way."

"Well, I usually work alone," said Cassius. "On the other
hand . . ."

In truth, the great salesman (who did have something of an
ego) was flattered by their request. Deep down, he had always
craved an appreciative audience for his performances.

"I suppose I could make use of a couple of assistants for a few
weeks," Cassius said with a smile.

So after persuading Cassius to stay the night, the three of them
left the next morning, zooming off on the carpet with new sets of
sample Wheels and Axles, eyes on the lookout for the next
Wheel customer.

In a matter of days, Max and Minnie began to see that what really made Cassius the Closer so terrific were four skills at which
he truly excelled.

First of all, Cassius was a master when it came to identifying
the relatively few people who were most likely to buy from him.

Today, this is known as "qualifying." It's a process of screening
the people available for the salesperson to contact so as to eliminate those who are unlikely to buy, and so that the attentions of
salesperson can be focused on the those who constitute the real
market.

You see, Cassius knew, and he accepted, that ninety-nine percent of the population was not going to buy the kinds of products
he sold. Either they didn't have the money or they couldn't envi-

sion the value of the product—or, often enough, the didn't have what it takes to break from the pack and try something totally new.

To make money, Cassius had to find that precious one percent who might buy. And he had to do it efficiently. There simply were not enough hours in the day for him to go around making sales pitches to everyone.

So how could he identify that one person out of the multitudes who was a true prospect for buying Wheels? Well, even though each individual customer was a new customer for him (someone he'd never met before), he was, in a sense, always looking for the same person.

Whether Cassius was selling Wheels, or flying carpets, or some other high-tech gizmo, most of his customers . . .

- Were wealthy enough to buy what he was selling
- Had the authority to make a risky decision
- Had the ego to want to be different from everyone else
- Were secure enough that think about the future (as opposed to having to spend all their energy dealing with today's problems)
- Were sufficiently resourceful that they did not need a lot of "handholding " from Cassius either before or after the sale

In addition to all of those traits, Cassius was also looking for people who shared one other critical characteristic. He wanted to find people who could see the product as being a tremendous opportunity. In the case of the Wheel, this meant people who stood to make a lot of money by moving things with this new technology.

Quite often, many of Cassius the Closer's customers were entrepreneurs like himself. Others were leaders of organizations, either large or small. Almost certainly they were people who did not need permission from others to make a commitment.

With those criteria in mind, Cassius would seek out his prospects. By simple observation, he could usually tell if he was in the right place, and if the person before him was even a candidate. If first impressions were favorable, he would then strike up a conversation. Often with just a few simple questions, he could determine very quickly whether the person was worth his time and energy.

Now, it's important to note that Cassius was charming and polite to everyone he met. He was a likable, charismatic guy, and almost everyone thought well of him.

But when Cassius was in selling mode, if he determined that someone did not meet the qualifications to being a customer, he would gracefully terminate the conversation and move on. He never squandered time on people who were not going to become customers.

On the other hand, once he found the right prospect—bingo.

The second selling skill of which Cassius the Closer was a master was the sales presentation—and at this he was second to none.

A presentation, of course, takes place when the salesperson shows or demonstrates the product to the customer. But when Cassius the Closer made a presentation, it was never a dry, rational affair. It was exciting, even dramatic. He always strove to show that the product he was selling would have a tremendous payoff for the customer.

And while many of his presentations were performed one-on-one—that is, between Cassius and one prospective customer—some were made to hundreds of people. These presentations went beyond being mere demonstrations of the Wheel; they were events.

One day, Max and Minnie were flying along with Cassius when they came to a city of some size.

"Well, this looks promising," said Cassius as they flew through the city gates.

"Who are we going to call on first?" asked Max.

"Nobody."

"Nobody?"

"You see, I've never been here before. So I have no leads."

"Then why did we come here?" asked Minnie. "How are you going to make any sales?"

"You just wait and see," said the great salesman.

Landing the flying carpet, he went straightaway to the city's new amphitheater, put down some cash, and rented the theater for the next day. Then he went to the forum and posted an ad, which read:

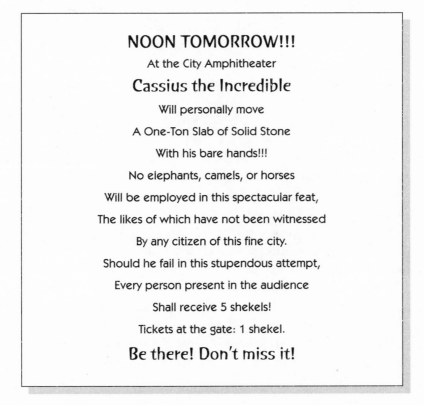

NOON TOMORROW!!!

At the City Amphitheater

Cassius the Incredible

Will personally move

A One-Ton Slab of Solid Stone

With his bare hands!!!

No elephants, camels, or horses

Will be employed in this spectacular feat,

The likes of which have not been witnessed

By any citizen of this fine city.

Should he fail in this stupendous attempt,

Every person present in the audience

Shall receive 5 shekels!

Tickets at the gate: 1 shekel.

Be there! Don't miss it!

The next day, by high noon, the seats at the amphitheater were filled to the top row.

Cassius took the stage and delivered a short, energetic introduction to build the excitement. Then he opened the curtain, and there, behind him onstage, was the one-ton slab of solid stone—mounted, naturally, on Max's Wheels and Axles.

To verify that the stone was as heavy as it looked, he invited volunteers from the audience to come onstage to try to lift it. After showing that they could not, Cassius signaled a fanfare of trumpets. Then he proceeded single-handedly to roll the big stone from one side of the stage to the next.

The audience was wowed.

Just to give them their money's worth, Cassius then piled other heavy objects on top of the stone—smaller stones, blocks of wood, sacks of grain—and rolled these easily about the stage as well. When the pile became too heavy for Cassius to move on his own, he invited the volunteers back, and together they pushed the load this way and that.

All the while, he talked about the tremendous gains that could be made possible by owning a Wheel.

Of course, some people in the audience were disappointed that Cassius had succeeded and they hadn't won the five shekels. But after the demonstration part of the event was over, many from the audience crowded around Cassius—who proceeded to make sales.

By charging a shekel a head at the gate, Cassius was able to make his own sales promotion pay for itself. He also had used the event not only to show the product, but to generate leads, too. And by the end of the afternoon, Cassius had sold every Wheel they had brought to town—and had taken orders for several dozen more besides.

"Hey," Cassius said afterward, toweling away the sweat of pushing stone slabs in the hot sun, "whatever it takes, I do."

A third skill at which Cassius truly excelled was this: Whenever a prospect began to resist the process of being sold a Wheel, Cassius kept 'em until they were customers. He did not allow prospects—and opportunities—to slip away.

Today, as then, this is known as "answering objections"—or, more accurately, as *resolving* objections.

Objections varied, but they were usually along the lines of "Well, let me think it over."

Or "Your Wheel is pretty cool, but . . . I don't know if I really need one."

Or "Man, I had no idea your Wheel thing would be so expensive!"

Cassius always took these kinds of statements in stride.

"Whenever I hear someone raise an objection," Cassius once said, "I always think to myself, I've almost got the sale."

"Almost got the sale?" asked Minnie. "How could you almost have the sale if someone doesn't want to buy?"

"Just because they raise an objection or two doesn't mean they don't want to buy," he said.

Cassius looked at objections as being *objects*. But much of the time, these objects, raised by the customer as a defense to hide behind, were not solid walls. They were more like doors. And Cassius felt it was his job as a salesman to find the key that would reopen that door.

One of the most common objections arose from the need for time.

"Let me sleep on it," the customer would say.

Unfortunately, Cassius could not afford that kind of time—for two reasons. First, he knew from experience that if he allowed the customer lots of time to think things over, the odds of making the sale were against him. Second, his own time was limited. If he had to wait and wait for one customer to make up his mind, that meant he was not able to sell to other customers in other places.

So when a prospect said something about "thinking it over," Cassius would indeed give them time. That is, he would give them an extra few minutes of his own—during which he would find out what was making them nervous.

"What objections really mean is that customers need something more," Cassius explained. "Maybe they need more information. Maybe they need assurance. Maybe they need to feel more excited. Or maybe they just need to feel they're getting a deal.

"Whatever is behind it, the objection is their way of slowing things down until they feel comfortable enough to proceed with the purchase. And it's my job to get them to that level of comfort—without letting them wander off and go to sleep."

The way Cassius handled objections was this:

First, he never argued. Because, if he did, he was the one who would lose.

Second, he was always sensitive to what the customer was saying—and to the feelings behind the customer's words. That did not mean he was passive or sympathetic. But only by being sensitive could he help the person get past the issues that were preventing the sale.

Third, he never supplied answers to the prospects' objections. He would use words to guide his prospects to their own answers.

Those were the three basic ground rules Cassius employed. The *process* he used for handling objections generally went like this:

- He would listen.
- He would repeat back to the person what he had heard the person say—not word for word, of course, but the general idea of what the person had said.
- He would ask the person to tell him more. In this way, he would get the person to reveal the true nature of the objection.

Sometimes he would have to repeat these steps one or two times until the heart of the matter became clear. Once the real issue was in the open, Cassius could—by using the third ground rule—help the prospect deal with it. This was the final step and the key to the whole process:

- He would guide the prospect into answering his own objection.

◆ ◆ ◆

One day, Cassius was demonstrating the Wheel to a local stone mason. Now, the mason clearly had a use for the Wheel, because he had to move lots of heavy stones almost every day on his job, and Cassius had already established that he could afford one.

But, shortly after Cassius mentioned the price, the mason stroked his chin and said, "Tell you what: let me think it over."

"You want to think it over? Okay, that's fine," said Cassius. "But could you help me with something first?"

"What's that?"

"Come on over here and sit down. This will take just a second."

They sat down, and Cassius leaned toward the mason and lowered his voice to a confidential tone.

"I was just hoping maybe you could tell me what part of the Wheel you're going to think about."

"Well, ah . . . I don't know."

"You see, if you could tell me what it is you need to think about it would sure help a lot."

"Why is that?"

"You see, it's my fault. After all, I'm only human. And it's obvious that when I explained how the Wheel works I left something out. Now, I know you're a busy guy, and here you're going to spend time— maybe even lose sleep—thinking about something that I should have explained better than I did."

Minnie's Notes . . .

Silence has been used for centuries as a closing technique. The game is simple. After asking a closing question, say nothing—because the person who speaks next loses.

"Oh, no, no!" said the mason. "That's not the problem. You explained everything real well. It's just that . . ."

Here, the mason paused, and Cassius knew to just listen and say nothing until the mason went on.

"It's just that . . . well, I'm not sure I really *need* the Wheel. And, after all, these things are kind of expensive."

"Okay, you're not sure you need one and you're concerned about the price."

"That's right." The mason began to stand up, but Cassius gently put a hand on his arm.

"Let me ask you this," said Cassius, "is your health important to you?"

"Sure it is," said the mason.

"And, like it or not, we're not getting any younger."

"True."

"And those stones you have to move every day, they're not getting any lighter."

"That's for darn sure."

"By the way, how's your back?"

The mason was a bit surprised, because he had not mentioned that, in fact, he had pulled a muscle in his back just a few days before. Cassius had taken a calculated guess that this was the case, having noticed that the mason was a bit stiff in his movements.

"Well, it's still a little sore, but it'll heal up."

"One thing about the Wheel, it's a back saver."

The mason nodded. "If I used Wheels, that would take a lot of physical wear and tear off of me, wouldn't it?"

"Absolutely," said Cassius.

The mason nodded a second time—but his face clouded suddenly. "Yeah, but . . . you're asking a lot of money for these Wheels."

"I won't argue with you," said Cassius. "They're not cheap. On the other hand, let me ask you this: How much money are you shelling out every time you have to visit the chiropractor?"

"Oh, maybe fifty shekels or so."

"Fifty?"

"Sometimes a hundred."

"A hundred shekels. Wow. Those fifties and hundreds have got to add up over time. And, as I say, we're not getting any younger. You might be going more than you have been."

The mason nodded once more and grimly.

"And what about the time you lose off the job?" asked Cassius. "That's got to cost you something."

"True. But I haven't lost that many days. I guess I've been kind of lucky."

"Well, for your sake, I hope you stay lucky. But what would happen if you did get behind on a job? Or on a couple of jobs?"

The mason just grunted, unwilling to invest any words in voicing what was secretly one of his worst fears.

At this point, Cassius switched tacks and went from the negative to the positive. "But, you know, with a Wheel, you could add to your business."

"Really?"

"Of course! You're going to be able to move more stones with less wear and tear on you. I would not be surprised if you could add fifty percent to your masonry business in the first year alone."

"So . . . I'll be making more income and saving my back?"

"More gain with less pain," Cassius confirmed.

The mason straightened up and looked past Cassius toward the horizon, where he seemed to see his future, bright and clear, revealed to him.

"I'd sure have the edge on the other masons in town, wouldn't I."

"That's right. While they're at the chiropractor, you'll be increasing your business."

The mason snapped to his feet, oblivious to the pinch of pain when he straightened, because his mind was racing forward. *I could underbid everyone else, take on more jobs, and still get the work done on time,* he was thinking. He went over to the Wheels, walked slowly around them with his hand stroking his chin and a certain fire in his eyes.

Cassius could not read the mason's mind, but he had a sense of what was going through it. He said casually, "You know, in a couple of years, with the gains made possible by the Wheel, you might even buy out some of your competition. You'd have those other masons working for you. You could even retire early."

The mason looked up, but he hardly saw the salesman. Inside his head, he was seeing himself on a river in small boat, a fishing line trailing in the water as he drifted lazily with the current.

"How much did you say you wanted for one of these Wheels?"

Bingo. Cassius the Closer, with his sense of timing, knew the door to the sale was open. The moment had come, and he was ready for the close.

The hallmark of Cassius the Closer was really that same skill he earned as part of his name: closing.

Closing was that part of the selling process in which the sale became a fact. It was the point at which prospects became customers, even if the money didn't change hands for a little while. Closing was when people to whom Cassius was pitching let go of their doubts and reservations and said yes.

Now, sometimes they didn't actually say "Yes" or "All right" or even "I'll take it." Sometimes they just gave a nod and smiled. Sometimes they asked for a firm delivery date. Sometimes they would ask a question like "These are going to be perfectly round when I get them, aren't they?" And Cassius would be the one to say, "Yes."

No matter. Whether they were jumping up and down with excitement or silently scribbling a signature, the common factor was that they had agreed to the sale.

Getting them to that point was, is, and always will be an art. There are hundreds, and quite possibly thousands, of closing techniques. Cassius knew about most of them. But as he once told Max and Minnie, "Every close I make stems from my ability to get the customer to feel either fear or desire—or a combination of the two."

"Fear?" Max wondered. Desire for a product—yes, he could understand how that could bring about a sale. But how could fear figure into it?

The simple answer was that Cassius would use the customer's fear of losing the opportunity to buy the product to make the sale.

In this way, Cassius, once he knew the prospect was hooked, would sometimes walk away. And the prospect would follow him!

Sometimes, if he knew a prospect really wanted a Wheel but was being difficult about the price, Cassius would actually *raise* the price. And the prospect, terrified that Cassius would raise the price still higher, would settle on the spot.

Nevertheless, perhaps because Cassius was fundamentally an optimist, he preferred to use closes based on desire—that is, desire along with its variants: greed and love.

When the stone mason said "How much did you say you wanted for these Wheels?" Cassius sensed he likely had the sale—so long as he closed it *now*—and that the one remaining obstacle was the mason's need to feel he was getting something off the asking price.

At least half of Cassius's customers, if not more, wanted the sense that they were not only getting a great, new, revolutionary product, but that they were also getting a deal on it.

Sometimes Cassius did not bargain at all. Sometimes, as previously mentioned, he would even raise the price—if he knew the prospect was truly hooked and was merely playing games with him.

But selling is an art, and Cassius, as the artist of the transaction, had learned to see each prospect individually and then paint the canvas accordingly.

In this case, he retold the price to the mason: "Twelve hundred shekels."

He said this firmly, sincerely. But the mason replied, "Gee, I'm not really sure I can afford that."

Cassius deliberately looked at the angle of the sun and said, "Well, I do have other appointments I have to make today."

"Um, maybe you could stop back tomorrow."

Cassius shook his head. "To be quite honest with you, I'm

booked tomorrow on a caravan headed south—if I haven't sold all my Wheels by the end of today, that is."

The mason's expression became concerned.

"Okay, here's what we'll do," said Cassius. "If we can agree on a price right now, will you buy a set of Wheels today?"

"Depends on the price," said the mason.

"Okay, then, why don't you make me a fair offer of what you'll pay?"

The mason lowered his gaze and began stroking his chin in earnest as he thought. Finally, he said, "A thousand shekels."

"A thousand? That's a genuine offer?"

"Yes, it is."

In fact, it so happened that 1,000 shekels was at the very low end of the range Cassius would accept. On rare occasions, he had been known to take 975. But since intuition told him that he pretty well had the mason committed at this point, Cassius did not accept that offer.

"Well, I'm sorry. I'd love to sell it to you for that price, and I know that might sound like a fair offer to you, but with our man-ufacturing costs being so high and demand for these things being so strong . . . I'd have to have more than that."

Now the mason was feeling the fear of loss. "Maybe I could go to eleven hundred."

Cassius bit his lip as if torn. He shook his head slowly—then suddenly relented. "I shouldn't do this, but you're a hardworking guy, and on account of your bad back, I guess I could live with eleven fifty."

The stone mason looked as if he had been given a reprieve from a harsh sentence. He extended his hand. "All right," he said. "It's a deal."

Minnie's Notes . . .

Bedrock Question #6

What added values does our salesperson have to offer to make a sale?

- Has to demonstrate the power and practicality of the technology
- Build the vision of the Wheel's potential for the customer
- Provide the emotional energy to close the sale

9

Sometimes, though, Max thought that Cassius the Closer was even a little too good. One day, he and Cassius were flying over the countryside when they found themselves in need of a snack. So they spotted a roadside stand where a farmer and several of his twelve kids were selling fruits and vegetables they grew on the surrounding land. The farmer's kids were dressed in ragged clothes, and it was clear that the farmer himself owned next to nothing beyond the dirt that grew his produce.

Naturally, the farmer was a bit surprised to see a flying carpet landing in front of his fruit stand, but he was even more interested in the Wheels that Cassius used as samples. (Flying carpets, after all, he had heard of; Wheels he had not.) So fascinated was the farmer that Cassius decided to strike up a conversation.

"What's your name?"

"Imum," said the farmer.

"Pleased to meet you. My name is Cassius."

"What are these things you've got with you?"

"These are called Wheels. Here, let me show you how they work."

Now, certainly this farmer would never have qualified for Cassius as being a normal customer. Yet it soon became obvious that Imum really wanted to own some Wheels—badly, in fact, because he offered all his fruits and vegetables for a pair.

The value of the produce, of course, came nowhere close to the actual price, and when Cassius did finally tell Imum how much a Wheel cost, the farmer was crestfallen.

Still, Cassius kept talking. And Imum kept talking to Cassius. And at the right moment, Cassius brought out a finance contract.

Always ready to close a sale, whatever it took, Cassius had pre-arranged credit with a bank back in town. The contract specified sky-high interest and penalties for paying late, but Imum barely looked at the terms. He signed the papers and, with a deep sigh of satisfaction and a smile on his face, took possession of his Wheels.

As they were leaving, Max said to Cassius, "How could you do that?"

"What? Did I do something wrong?"

"That's guy's got all those kids to feed! He's probably going to lose his farm trying to make the payments on that contract he just signed!"

"Look," said Cassius, turning Max toward Imum, who was gleefully rolling his Wheels across the fields to show his wife (who was probably going to be less than thrilled). "Look at him! Half an hour ago, that guy was nobody. He had nothing but dirt. And he knew it.

"But now he's one of the few people on the face of the Earth who owns his own Wheels. *Now* he's spe-

Minnie's Notes . . .

Closers have a remarkable—and sometimes unfortunate—ability to put the sale ahead of all other considerations. Many can operate without feelings of guilt that would be normal in other people.

cial. *Now,* for once in his life, he's somebody. And he knows it, too.

"Will he be able to come up with the payments? I don't know! But you see, I didn't just sell that farmer a Wheel; I sold him the opportunity to be better than the nobody he was. And he bought it—because the risk of losing his farm tomorrow was far outweighed by the alternative of being a nobody for the rest of his life."

Then, leaving the farmer and his family to whatever their fate might be, they flew onward to the next city, Max still feeling vaguely guilty about the sale, while Cassius the Closer felt no guilt whatsoever.

Yet you could not fault Cassius on the basis of results. Before long, Max and Minnie found that their bank account was full of money and their house was empty of Wheels.

Max had to quit going on sales calls so he could turn out more Wheels for Cassius to sell. Soon, he even had to quit making the Wheels in his home workshop. It was too small to handle the demand. He rented a much larger workshop up the street, and he even hired helpers to assist him.

One morning Max and Minnie had to go across town to meet with their accountant, and they came upon a crowd of people who were lining both sides of the street.

Max tapped one of the spectators on the shoulder and asked, "What's going on? Some kind of parade?"

"They're bringing in one of the new obelisks," said the spectator.

Sure enough, there came toward them on the street one of the longest and biggest pieces of cut stone that the world had ever seen. And as it passed by, Max saw to his great satisfaction and surprise that they were using his Wheels to move it.

"Hey, what are those round things underneath?" the spectator asked.

Insights from Ozzie the Oracle . . .

Top Characteristics of a World Class Closer

- Entrepreneurial outlook. Always has an eye on what might become the "next wave."
- A strong track record of selling new concepts.
- Focuses on selling the kinds of breakthrough products and services that generate real excitement—yet don't require a lot of personal attention from the closer after the sale.
- Seemingly born with an instinct for sales, but also has excellent learned sales skills, particularly with respect to qualifying, presenting, resolving objections, and closing.
- High energy level. A polished, sophisticated demeanor. The "look of success."
- Keeps personal sales efficiency high by using personal assistants (and technology) to manage the nitty-gritty.
- Most develop their salesmanship with the help of a mentor, who teaches them the skills and attitudes for success.
- Common liability: a capacity for operating unconstrained by feelings of responsibility for what happens to the customer as a consequence of the sale.

Max told him.

"Pretty clever," said the spectator.

"Thank you," said Minnie. "My husband invented them."

"Go on! Really?"

"It's true."

"Well, if it is, you sure did everybody a favor. They're talking about putting up these obelisks all over the place."

"And that's just the beginning," said another of the spectators. "I heard that now that they can move big heavy stones, they're going to be building all kinds of new monuments—plus palaces, temples, tombs, you name it. And you know what that means? Lots of good-paying construction jobs."

"Yeah," said the first spectator, "and just think about what it'll do for tourism!"

Max and Minnie beamed with pride. Their hard work had paid off. The Wheel had *arrived*.

The future could not have seemed brighter.

Minnie's Notes . . .

What Does It Mean to Be "World Class"?

Being designated as "World Class" indicates that a salesperson or a sales force sets the standard for being the best of its kind. World Class sales forces establish and observe professional best practices that yield superior results in terms of sales revenue and customer satisfaction.

Part Two

THE WHEEL
ADVANCES

10

The months passed. Cassius by now was traveling constantly, and each trip seemed to take him farther and farther afield in his search for new customers for the Wheel.

Then one day there came a knock on the Wheel Workshop door. Max opened it to find Cassius standing before him.

"Well, well!" said Max. "Come in, come in! Hey, Minnie, look who's here!"

"Cassius! Good to see you!" said his wife. "Did you just get in?"

"Yeah, just got back from Egypt," said the great salesman.

"Really? How are they coming along with the Pyramid?" Max asked.

"You mean the first Pyramid? Oh, it's finished. But now they're working on a new one—even bigger than the first! In fact, they're going to call it the Great Pyramid, and it's going to be *enormous*."

"No kidding," said Max.

"And actually, that's the reason I dropped by," said Cassius.

"Why don't you both sit down. I've got some great news . . . and some not-so-great news."

"What's going on?" asked Max.

"I'll give you the great news first. I just closed the biggest Wheel sale *ever*."

"Really? That's terrific! Tell us about it."

"Okay. I was in Egypt, and I got a message from . . . well, you're hardly going to believe who, but take a guess."

"I don't know. The sun god?"

"Close! Very close! I met with . . . *the Pharaoh*."

"No! King Khufu himself?"

"In the flesh," said Cassius. "He's a great guy, by the way. Terrific sense of humor. Anyway . . . turns out he's a gadget freak! And he's been hearing about the Wheels his stone vendors have been using to move their stone from their quarries over to Giza, where they're building the new Pyramid. So I gave His Maj a demonstration of the Wheel—and he went gaga! Brought in his chief engineer on the Great Pyramid project—whose first objection was that they had bought hundreds of new sledges to move the big stones around. But we talked it over, and it turned out that you, Max, are going to supply the Wheels to *retrofit* all of their sledges!"

"Really? What do you mean by 'retrofit'?"

"By drilling holes through the runners of each sledge, you can then push Axles through the runners and attach Wheels. It was the chief engineer's idea. Stroke of genius, I thought. Let me think, what was his name? Umm . . ." Cassius snapped his fingers. "Mr. Cobra."

"Mr. Cobra?"

"Yeah, that was his name. You'll like him. Very bright man. Anyway, with two Axles and four Wheels for each sledge, it's going to be a very lucrative contract."

"Huh," said Max. "Well, it sounds good, but . . . you know, it's never been done before. I sure hope there aren't any problems."

"Problems?! *Nah!* Why would there be any problems?"

"How much is the contract worth?" Minnie asked.

"That's why I suggested you both sit down," said Cassius. "Are you ready for this? One . . . *million* . . . shekels."

Max and Minnie dropped their jaws, looked wide-eyed at each other, and then became giddy with glee.

"Whoa! A million!"

"You did say one *million* shekels?"

"Yep. One of the biggest sales of my career," Cassius said with a grin.

"Okay, what's the not-so-great news?" asked Minnie.

"Well, it's just that I also came to say good-bye."

"You're leaving?"

"It's time for me to seek fresher pastures."

"How can that be? You just said you closed one of the biggest sales of your career."

"True, but the reality is that I've sold about as many Wheels as I'm going to be able to sell around here. Each trip I make gets longer and longer. And, as you might or might not know, a flying carpet has only so many hours of flying time before it has to be recharged, and mine is running a little low at this point. If I have to lug those Wheels around by camel or donkey or whatever, I'll never make any real money! Anyway, the cherries have all been picked. It's time to move on."

> ## Minnie's Notes . . .
>
> It's fairly common for closers to change the products they sell every few years. Often, it's because they have by then hit all the "new" customers who are likely to buy from them.

The excitement that Max and Minnie had been feeling now turned to shock.

"Look, we've done each other a world of good," said Cassius. "And as I travel through foreign lands and meet with various merchants, kings, and emperors, I'll certainly mention the Wheel—and if I can make a sale big

enough to justify the shipping and travel hazards, I'll send a messenger with the down payment, and you can handle it from there.
Sound good?"

"I don't know," said Max, "I thought we'd be working together
for some time to come."

"Hey, it's been a few years now. Nothing lasts forever, you know."

"Well, if that's your decision. . . ."

"Good luck to you," said Minnie.

They settled their accounts and bid each other farewell.

In parting, Cassius said, "And listen, Max, if you keep inventing and come up with the next big thing, you be sure to get word
to me, okay?"

"Will do," said Max.

Cassius stepped onto his magic carpet, which was laden with
several trunks full of shekels. He clapped his hands. The carpet
rose into the air, and Cassius the Closer flew off into the sunset.

"I guess we'll have to find another closer," Minnie said to Max
over dinner.

"Yeah. I guess we will. But, hey, he got us a million shekels in
business. That'll keep us busy for a while."

For the next few weeks, Max and his helpers worked very hard.
Finally, they had the first batch of Wheels and Axles ready for delivery. Max personally escorted the first shipment on the caravan
to the Great Pyramid construction site, and showed them to the
chief engineer, Mr. Cobra.

"Well, here are your Wheels," said Max. "I'll have the next
batch ready for you in a month. Thanks for your business. We
certainly appreciate it."

And he turned to leave.

But Mr. Cobra said, "Wait a minute. Where do you think
you're going?"

"Back to work. I've got to make more Wheels for you."

"You're just going to leave these things in front of my tent and walk away?"

"Um, would you like me to leave them someplace else?"

"I expect these Wheels to be *installed*."

Max's mouth dropped open. "Installed? You mean, you want them put on the sledges?"

"That's right. Didn't that salesman of yours tell you that?"

"Well, he said something, but it was kind of vague."

"Then let me be clear," said Mr. Cobra. "I expect these Wheels to be delivered *and* installed on time. And furthermore, I expect total support."

"Total support? What do you mean by that?"

"Come over here," said Mr. Cobra, beckoning to Max. And they went behind the tent, where a vast vista of activity spread before them. There were the multitudes of workers wielding hammers and chisels, huge blocks of stone, piles of sand and dirt, elephants and camels, and the rudimentary foundation of what might someday be the Great Pyramid.

"Take a look," said the engineer. "I've got thousands of workers on this job. They don't know Wheels from donuts. If they're not *trained* in how to use these Wheels, we're going to have accidents. People are going to get hurt. My insurance is going to go up. Our productivity will likely go down. And if we don't stay on schedule, heads will roll. Got the picture?"

"Yes, but . . . I thought we just had to supply the Wheels."

"Hey, we're paying you people top shekel. Those Wheels are useless unless they're installed correctly and the workers know how to use them. If you can't provide those things, the deal is off."

Max knew he was in a jam. He definitely did not want to lose the Great Pyramid contract.

"All right, look," he told Mr. Cobra. "I'll take care of it. But you've got to give me a few days to make arrangements."

"Fair enough," said the chief engineer.

◆   ◆   ◆

His stomach churning, Max came to the scary conclusion that with the Great Pyramid project, something fundamental in the selling process had changed. With a big job like this, things were not as simple as just closing the sale, delivering the order, and moving on. Things were getting complex. They weren't just selling a product anymore.

When he got home, he told Minnie what Mr. Cobra had said.

"Minnie, I've still got hundreds of Wheels to build. You've got to step in and help with this."

"Me? What about Cassius? He's the salesman. Isn't this kind of thing partly his job?"

"Hah! Cassius has already collected his commission. Who knows where he is by now."

"So send a marathon runner with a message! Get him back here!"

Max shook his head. "Even if we track him down, what good would that do? He doesn't know how to train workers. He's not going to get down in the sand and figure out how to do a retrofit. As far as he's concerned, he's done his job. He closed the sale. He figures it's up to us to take care of 'little details' like putting them on and teaching the workers how to use the darn things."

"But, Max, I don't know anything about putting Wheels on sledges! And how do you expect *me* to go about training thousands of workers?"

"Hey, we're in this together, dear. You'll just have to do the best you can," said her husband. "Look, I'll give you my best helper, Artemus. Have him figure out the retrofit part of it, and you deal with the rest."

"All right," she said reluctantly. "I'll try."

But after a few days, Minnie came home on the verge of tears.

"Max, there's no way! One of Mr. Cobra's engineers gave Artemus some drawings of the sledge, but Artemus didn't know what to make of them—he doesn't know how to read an engineering drawing."

"Okay, okay. I'll take some time off and go out there."

"It gets worse, Max! When it comes to training and support, they don't just want me to show them how the Wheel works, they expect me to tell them how to move these big stones!"

"Huh? What do you mean?" asked Max.

"I thought I could go out there and say 'Here's a Wheel, and here is how it goes 'round and 'round,' and that kind of thing. But Mr. Cobra expects me to tell them things like how much weight the Wheel will support. His staff wants me to calculate optimum loads. They want to know stopping distances for a given tonnage. They expect me to specify the tensile strength of the rope they need to use."

"Holy moley! Even I don't know half of that stuff."

"And," said his wife, "they want a maintenance schedule—plus, I think they expect us to supply someone to *do* the maintenance. The way Mr. Cobra put it, they want a total solution."

Max stroked his chin. "We've really got a problem. We need somebody in Giza who really knows what's what. Someone who can solve problems and work with Cobra's engineers. But if I don't stay here and keep turning out Wheels, we'll never meet the terms of the contract. I don't know what to do."

Just then, there was a knock at the door. Max opened it to find Ben the Builder smiling and extending a hand in greeting. This, in fact, was not the first time Ben had visited; every three to six months since they had parted ways, Ben had found some occasion to come by and say hello.

"How's it going?" asked Ben.

"Well, ah . . . so-so," said Max.

"Listen, I was just passing by and I wanted to see if you two could use a couple of tickets to the Gladiators match next week."

"Oh, well, that's very thoughtful of you," said Minnie. "But, to tell you the truth, we're so busy I don't think we could use them if we wanted to."

"Business is *that* good?" asked Ben.

"Kind of," said Max.

"Hey, is there a problem?" Ben asked. "Anything I might help you with?"

Max and Minnie looked at each other. Then Max said, "Thanks, Ben, nice of you to offer, but I don't think so."

Ben accepted this, then he chitchatted a minute about what he'd been up to lately, worked in a couple of the latest Sphinx jokes that were then making the rounds, and was on his way.

After he had left, Minnie turned to Max and posed a question: "Are you sure we couldn't . . . ?"

Max shook his head. "He's a great guy and everything, but he doesn't understand the technical end."

All of a sudden, Minnie's face brightened. "Wait a minute! What about Toby?"

"Toby who?"

"You remember—Toby. The one who's the licensed wizard."

Max snapped his fingers. "Oh, yeah! You're right. She's smart. She could figure out the retrofit problem, and maybe all the rest of it. Do we know how to get hold of her?"

"Let me see if I still have her résumé."

Minnie's Notes . . .

For <u>wizard</u> you can substitute a professional expert of any stripe—engineer, accountant, lawyer, architect, doctor, etc. These salespeople use their sophisticated technical knowledge to help customers make the right decisions.

An hour later, Max and his wife were rushing across town. They found the address, knocked on the door, and, much to their relief, Toby appeared.

"Well, hello!" said the Wizard. "It's been a long time. Won't you come in?"

After they sat down, she said, "I hear the Wheel is really going places these days."

"Yes, we're doing just fine," said Minnie. "How about you? Did you find a job?"

"Yes, I did. I'm working on one of the new obelisks. But they just have me helping with the engineering details. Doing the drawings. That kind of thing."

Max came straight to the point. "What would you think about coming to work for us again?"

"Well, ah . . . I'm not sure. It didn't work out very well the last time."

"We think this would be different," said Minnie. "We'd like you to help us on the Great Pyramid job."

"Seriously? The Great Pyramid!" Toby the Wizard was ecstatic. "But . . . would you want me to sell for you?"

"You would be working with the customer," said Max, "mostly with the chief engineer, but also with a lot of the managers—and even some of the royal court. Your job would be to supervise installing the Wheels we deliver and to help them integrate the Wheel into their day-to-day work routine."

Toby nodded. "But what would you pay me?"

Max looked at Minnie. With a million shekels at stake, they could afford to pay for contingencies like a wizard or two.

"Whatever you're making now," Minnie said, "we'll double it."

"And," added Max, remembering what she had said some time before in her interview, "if you do well, we'll consider a career track into Wheel management."

"All right, then," said Toby. "You've hired yourselves a wizard."

Minnie's Notes . . .

Compensation for a wizard salesperson is often just salary, rather than commission, but coupled with the potential for advancement (and possibly perks like stock options).

11

So Toby went to work.

She made it her first priority to go to the Great Pyramid herself and sit down with Mr. Cobra—who proceeded to vent his many frustrations over these expensive yet, so far, useless Wheels he had been stuck with.

He was angry and sometimes loud, but Toby did not argue with him. Instead, she listened, she took lots of notes, and she responded as best she could to all the issues he raised.

How soon would the sledges have their Wheels?

"I have my people working on it now. We should have the first one fitted with Wheels the day after tomorrow. We'll then run it through some tests, and if it passes, we should be able to do one sledge a week, maybe more."

When were the pyramid workers to be trained?

"Here, I've already put together a schedule."

What kind of rope should they be using?

"I recommend a bronze-wire and camel-hair interweave with a minimum draw strength of three megastones."

What about optimum loads?

"Why don't I sit down with your engineers after the tests and we'll do the calculations."

What about stopping distances for a given tonnage? What about all the other technical stuff they needed?

"I'll put together a manual with all that information."

When?

"You'll have it in six weeks."

We need it by the end of the month.

"No problem. I'll take care of it."

Almost as vexing to Mr. Cobra as all the other issues combined was the matter of Cassius the Closer. He was the one who had sold them the Wheels; why wasn't he around to take care of the details of the sale?

To this Toby said, "From now on, I will be on hand. Whatever your concerns about the Wheel, talk to me. If I'm not on-site, I'll be sure that a messenger knows where to reach me."

So it came to pass that when the pyramid workers moved the very first stones by Wheel, Toby was on hand. Which was a good thing, because having never done this before, the pyramid workers had plenty of questions for which no one had a ready answer.

Time after time, Mr. Cobra and his engineers had to consult with Toby in order to figure out the best thing to do.

Even after they began to get the stones rolling, there were plenty of other worries.

She had to coordinate the delivery of the remaining Wheels under contract. In fact, one of her many roles was to communicate the customer's special requests back to Max and Minnie. By being on-site much of the time, she was able to notice certain problems and deficiencies in the Wheel's original design—and she had the technical savvy to come up with solutions.

One afternoon, two of the Wheels cracked. Mr. Cobra and his staff fretted mightily over the possible delays this would mean. But because of Toby, replacements were expedited to the site, and work at the Great Pyramid stayed on schedule.

Then there was Wheel maintenance. That, too, was one of Toby's responsibilities. You see, in those days, there was no Wheel infrastructure. That is, you couldn't just roll your Wheel down to the corner garage to have it serviced—as, of course, there were no corner garages. So Toby had to interview, hire, and train people to perform the maintenance chores at the Great Pyramid construction site.

Indeed, from this maintenance effort came one of many firsts in Wheel history: the first time grease was ever applied to silence a squeaky Wheel. Decades of careful scholarship have established without question that this was Toby's idea.

Just when Toby thought she had everything under control, who should come buzzing by the Great Pyramid? Yes—it was none other than Cassius the Closer.

He claimed he was just passing through and thought he would see how things were coming along. Actually, he was in a slump. He had picked up a new product to sell: magic lamps, the kind with genies inside. But quality control was not very good; sometimes the genie appeared and sometimes the genie didn't. Customers were not amused at the latter result.

To make matters worse, his flying carpet manufacturer had gone out of business, forced into bankruptcy by liability lawsuits. So Cassius thought he might change his fortunes by returning to Wheels. His plan was to head eastward and perhaps sell them in India and maybe even China. And as the Great Pyramid was more or less on his way, he thought he might just as well stop by to see if any opportunities presented themselves.

"You must be Toby," he said, stepping off his magic carpet. "I've heard of you through Max and Minnie, but I don't believe we've ever met. I am Cassius the Closer."

"Yes, I've heard of you, too. What a surprise!"

Toby smiled pleasantly, though in fact she was not exactly thrilled to see him. After all, she had been working month after month, and often for long hours, to keep the pyramid builders happy. Now here came Cassius, returning like a prodigal son. Was he there to reclaim her customer as his own?

> **Minnie's Notes . . .**
>
> Closers are subject to streaks and slumps. The nature of their businesses is such that they have to make large bets on risky ventures, and sometimes those bets fail to pay off. Sometimes they run hot and seem invincible, and sometimes they slump so deep that their former glories fade.

She need not have worried.

Cassius led the way to Mr. Cobra's tent and charmed his way inside, but the reception was not what he might have hoped for.

"Oh, yeah," said Mr. Cobra. "Cassius the Closer. You were off in the wild blue yonder last I heard."

After making pleasantries, Cassius proceeded to regale them with some Spartan jokes he'd picked up in Athens, but it soon became clear that he was going to try to sell them Wheels—or anything else.

Mr. Cobra stopped him cold. "It is true that we might have a need for a few more Wheels, but not the kind you sold us. We already have enough of those."

"What other kinds of Wheels might you be needing?" asked Cassius.

"Max and I are custom designing some innovative new Wheel systems," Toby explained. "We'll be using much larger diameters than ever before, and we'll be joining them in tandem pairs."

"Yes, for the truly monumental stones we need to move," added Mr. Cobra. "By the way, Toby, how is that coming along?"

"It's looking very positive. We should be starting the field testing next week."

"Excellent!" said Cobra. "Now, what about the cracking problem you were having?"

"I think we have that solved," she said, and continued to go over the technicalities of the project in some detail—all of which held Mr. Cobra's rapt interest.

It was not long before it became clear to Cassius the Closer that he was not going to earn any commissions there.

Graciously, he excused himself from the discussion, saying "Well, I'm off to India. Good luck finishing the Great Pyramid."

"Nice meeting you," said Toby. "Have a nice trip."

No, Toby the Wizard would never be a gifted closer like Cassius. Yet she had become the one with whom the customer preferred to do business.

Toby had won Mr. Cobra's confidence. She knew her stuff, she got things done, and she was especially competent at managing the details that closers like Cassius left behind for others to deal with. And with customers like Mr. Cobra, those were the things that mattered.

One day, down at the Wheel Workshop, there came a knock at the door. Max put down his hammer and chisel and stepped away from the block of stone he was so carefully rounding into a finished product. He opened the door to find a man whose face brightened into a big smile at the sight of the famous Wheelmaker.

"Well, I've found you at last!"

"I guess so," said Max. "What can I do for you?"

"I just want to say thank-you." The man took Max's hand and pumped it up and down. "Thank you for creating the Wheel and changing my life."

"You're welcome," said Max, now looking closely and somewhat suspiciously at the man. "But . . . have we met before?"

"Have we met? You bet we've met! Though I have to say I don't know that you'd remember. It was quite a while ago. I was selling vegetables grown on my farm from a stand by the side of the road when you and that salesman came along and sold me some Wheels."

"Oh, yeah, I do remember you now," said Max.

The man extended his hand once more. "Imum's the name."

"Right. How do you do. Won't you come inside?"

They stepped into the workshop, and Imum, still beaming, looked around at all the Wheels in various stages of production.

"Well, well. I finally get to see where your famous Wheels are made," said Imum.

"Yep, they all come out of here," said Max. "So how's everything going for you?"

"Just fine. Couldn't be better. Say, is that salesman around?"

"You mean Cassius the Closer?"

"That's the name! Cassius."

"Sorry, but he's traveling right now."

"That's too bad. I did want say hello."

"Whenever I see him again, I'll tell him you stopped by," said Max. "So . . . you say the Wheel changed your life?"

"It sure did."

"I guess it made your farm a lot more productive and enabled you and your family to earn a decent living."

"Oh, heck no," Imum said. "About a month after we bought it, one of those Wheels you sold us cracked in two. We ended up losing the farm. Couldn't make the payments."

Afraid now of what Imum might be up to, Max took a step backward. "Gee, I'm very sorry to hear that."

"Yeah, I was sorry, too. It was awful. I couldn't sleep nights, what with worrying about how we were going to survive."

"Listen, maybe I could build you another Wheel, since one of yours broke."

"No, no, you don't need to do that," said Imum. "See, one of those nights I couldn't sleep I got to looking at the pieces of that broken Wheel. And I got to thinking, 'You know, I could probably build one of these myself.' I'm pretty handy with mechanical stuff, being a farmer and all. So I set to it, and in just two or three days, I'd done it."

"Done what?"

"I'd built my own Wheel."

"Really? You built your own? In a couple of days?"

"Right. Of course, I can do it much faster now, since I know what I'm doing."

Max was highly doubtful of this, because it took him much longer than that to craft a Wheel.

"Come on outside," said Imum. "I'll show you."

Max followed the farmer through the door and just around the corner. Imum gestured to the strangest contraption Max had ever seen.

"What the heck is that?"

"I call it the Wheelbarrow."

"The Wheelbarrow? Huh. It looks like a big wooden box set on top of a Wheel that's . . . say, wait a minute." Max got down on his hands and knees to look closely. "This Wheel isn't made out of stone."

"No, it's not," said Imum. He rapped his knuckles—*thunk, thunk*—against it. "I made it out of wood."

Max straightened up and put his hands on his hips. "Wood? Why would you ever want to make a Wheel out of wood?"

"Well, I didn't have any good stone, so I just used what was available. Besides, I happen to think my Wheelbarrow Wheels are *better* than what you sold me."

"And why is that?"

"Because wooden Wheels are lighter and easier to handle. It doesn't take as much effort to turn them. And if they break, they can be repaired. If one of your stone Wheels breaks, as I know from experience, it's history."

With a skeptical face, Max walked slowly around the strange-looking Wheelbarrow. "So . . . what do you use this thing for?"

"As you can see, I load it up with fresh produce from my farm. I push the Wheelbarrow into the city, and then I sell the produce—

and for very good prices. I can reach more customers, and I sell a lot more vegetables than I used to from my roadside stand."

"I thought you said you'd lost your farm."

"I did. But after I built my Wheelbarrow, I started hauling things for other farmers. Before long, I'd made enough to buy back the farm. In fact, I'm making so much money from hauling the produce and selling it, I don't do the actual farming anymore. I pay other people to do that. I've got four other Wheelbarrows like this one, and my family and I have built a nice business out of hauling vegetables. And you know what? I've even had offers from other people asking me to build Wheelbarrows for them."

"No kidding," said Max. "Well . . ." He stuck out his hand for Imum to shake. "I'm glad everything worked out for you. Good luck in the future."

"Thanks. But I've got to give you the credit," Imum said. "You were a pioneer, Max. You got the whole Wheel thing rolling. If it weren't for you, I'd still be muckin' around in the dirt."

With that, Imum hefted his Wheelbarrow and started off down the street. "So long!"

"Bye," said Max.

As he watched the Wheelbarrow turn the far corner, Max shook his head and said to himself, "Wheelbarrows . . . hah! They'll never catch on. And who would ever want a Wheel made out of wood when they can get a quality, heavy-duty Wheel crafted from the finest marble?"

He turned, went back inside his shop, got back to work, and tried to forget about Imum and his silly Wheelbarrow.

Trouble was, he could not.

In fact, Max began to worry. No, the Wheelbarrow with its ridiculous single Wheel was no threat, he felt. On the other hand, what if Imum came up with some kind of giant Wheelbarrow capable of moving big stones?

And even if Imum stuck with hauling vegetables, Max had an even bigger worry: the Great Pyramid project would soon be coming to an end.

Yes, the Pharaoh and his heirs would be building these great piles of stone for some time to come. But the job of putting Wheels on all the sledges was almost finished. Max and his helpers were crafting the last batch.

Of course, there still would be maintenance and add-on sales, like those special heavy-duty Wheel systems Toby had been working on. But the sum of it all wasn't going to total anything close to a million shekels.

Anyway, aside from that, deep in his gut, Max felt that they were missing an opportunity. The Great Pyramid project, big as it had been, was surely only the beginning. Instead of merely a million shekels, they might be earning many millions—if they could find more customers.

Yes, that was it. All of Max's worries pointed to this: They needed more customers. New customers.

Yet Cassius had gone off to China. And Toby? True, she had done well. But could she go out on her own and bring back business? Max was anything but convinced she could.

One evening after work, Max was pacing his living room, worrying and thinking, thinking and worrying, when Minnie came and asked, "What would you like for dinner, dear?"

Suddenly it came to Max what they should do.

"Something special," Max said to her. "Something very special."

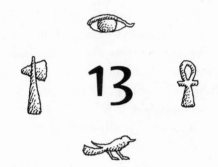

13

Following a delicious pâté of ground camel and goat curd came the soup, a Red Sea seafood bisque.

Next, a salad of exotic greens gathered from the banks of the Tigris River and said to have wisdom-enhancing powers.

At last, the main course: roast rack of lamb, basted with the finest olive oil and herbs, done crisp on the outside and medium rare on the inside.

Stuffed, the Oracle reclined on his favorite rock and said, "Well, you two must be doing quite well to put together a gourmet offering like that."

"To tell you the truth," said Max, "we had it catered."

"But we are doing well," Minnie added. "Our Wheels are helping to build the Great Pyramid, and we've got lots of shekels in the bank."

"So what's the problem?" asked the Oracle.

"Our problem is that good things come to an end," said Max.

And he told the Oracle everything that was on his mind, about the Great Pyramid project coming to an end, about Imum and the Wheelbarrow, about Cassius going to China, and about Toby the Wizard.

Half an hour later, after Max had told him everything that was bugging him, the Oracle asked again, "So what's the problem?"

"Isn't it obvious? We need more customers," said Max, "and we don't have anyone to sell for us!"

"What's wrong with Toby?"

"Well . . ."

"She's very good at handling the technical stuff," said Minnie, "but we don't know if she can sell to new customers."

"She didn't do very well when we first started the business," Max added.

"Hey, when you first got into the business," said the Oracle, "the market was different. In fact, there was no market. You had to create one—using the energy, the drive, the vision, and the tremendous skills of a closer like Cassius. But now things have changed."

"Have they?" asked Max. "We're still selling Wheels."

"Yes, but, Max, think about this: Why did Cassius leave?"

"He said he was leaving because he had already sold Wheels to everyone around here who was going to buy them."

"Then why don't you just close down the company?" asked the Oracle.

Max was silent.

"Because," said the Oracle, answering for him, "you know in your heart there are tons more Wheels to be sold. But they won't be sold by Cassius. His kind of customers have dried up."

"His kind?"

"Look at the people who bought from him: opportunists buying a piece of tomorrow, buying a dream. Yet look, too, at the terms: In exchange for the opportunity, the first owners of the Wheel were willing to buy the technology 'as is' and adapt it to their own needs. They didn't need training; they would teach

themselves how to use the Wheel. Didn't care about maintenance; they'd figure that out on their own. However, there is always a limited supply of these pioneers, these adventurers. When
that supply dwindled, Cassius moved on.

"Now, though, as you learned at the Great Pyramid, there are
other kinds of customers. Only they don't want just a Wheel.
They don't want just an opportunity. They can see the benefit of
the Wheel, but they want you to supply everything.

"Think about it in terms of my favorite subject—food. If Cassius had been selling a meal, he'd have been providing the raw
meat or fish or whatever for the main course, and he'd have told
customers how good it would be once they cooked it right. Mr.
Cobra and customers of his kind want the whole meal, from ap-
petizer to soup and salad to the entrée and even the dessert. Furthermore, they want it cooked for them by an expert chef. And
they're willing to foot the bill.

"That's your market now: customers who want the whole meal.
You're not just selling Wheels anymore. You're selling Wheels
and the service to put these Wheels onto a sledge, and training,
and maintenance—and above all, the expertise that guarantees
the customer will get the expected results. In short, as your Mr.
Cobra put it, you're selling a total solution."

"Yes, but how many more Great Pyramid jobs are there in the
world?" asked Minnie.

"There might not be other pyramids, but there will be other
customers who need that level of support. And Toby can win
those sales. Don't forget that because of the Great Pyramid job
you now have the credibility to go to anyone, anywhere, and say,
'No matter how big the job, no matter how complicated, we can
handle it.' "

Max was skeptical. "I just can't see Toby going out there and
closing sales the way Cassius did."

"No, because she won't sell like Cassius. She'll do it her own
way. And you're going to have to be patient. Closers either make
or lose the sale in one or two contacts with the customer. Toby's

kind of sale is more complex and requires a higher level of trust—usually about six to nine months from first contact until the sale is closed."

"You see," said Minnie, "that was the problem the first time around. Toby took too long."

"Yes, but now," said the Oracle, "you should have enough shekels in the bank to last until the next sale, if you budget them with care."

Max thought this over. "This is very different from the way we started out."

"Let me show you something," said the Oracle.

He went to the back of the cave and returned with an ancient scroll. He unrolled it next to the fire for Max and Minnie to see.

"These are the Nine Steps of Selling," said the Oracle. "This is the whole cycle—from first contact through the first sale and on to making repeat sales. But do you notice anything?"

Max and Minnie studied the scroll. Finally, Minnie said, "Cassius never had to bother with a lot of these steps."

"That is exactly right," said the Oracle. "A closer focuses on steps three through six, from qualifying through closing the sale. Everything else gets only the minimum of his attention and energy."

"Why?" asked Max.

"Because that's how he stays efficient. But you, on the other hand, for the foreseeable future, have to be concerned about all nine steps. If you aren't, your credibility will go up in smoke, and you'll be history."

"Okay, but can we make as much money as before?" asked Max.

"An excellent question," said the Oracle. "And the answer is a qualified yes. You can make as much profit—and more—in this kind of market, provided that you adjust your prices and manage expenses in keeping with the complexity of the sale. Remember, you're not just selling Wheels anymore, you're selling total solutions in which Wheels are merely the key component."

The Nine Steps of Selling . . .

Marketing

1. *Marketing Communications.* The idea here is to build an image that will induce the right kind of attention and cause people to take an interest in you.
2. *Generating Leads.* Hand in hand with creating the impression is encouraging contacts with specific people who might become customers.
3. *Qualifying Prospects.* A matter of separating the wheat from the chaff, of not wasting your time on those who do not have the means or the need to buy from you.

Sales

4. *Presentation.* The salesperson's pitch. The phase in which the salesperson tailors the capabilities being offered to the specific needs and desires of the individual who might buy.
5. *Resolving Objections.* In which the prospect does the hemming and hawing and tries to say "I'll think about it," and the salesperson uses that hemming and hawing to remove the final barriers to the sale.
6. *Closing the Sale.* The act—and art—of persuading the customer to say yes.

Service

7. *Execution and Service.* Managing the fulfillment of the terms of the sale in such a way that the customer is satisfied, both now and later.
8. *Building Relationships.* Personal contacts that take place after the first sale between the customer and the salesperson or the company or, preferably, both.
9. *Repeat Business.* The pot of gold at the end of the rainbow, the reason for taking such trouble to deliver great service and build relationships.

"But we can't sell total solutions to just anybody," said Minnie. "That's going to be very expensive."

"You know, it must be my influence," said the Oracle. "You two are getting much smarter the longer you hang out with me.

"You're exactly right. Not everyone wants a total solution—and certainly not everyone can afford one. A big chunk of your job as Toby's manager is going to be making sure that she stays focused on the prospects that offer the most upside potential. You want medium to big orders—and customers. If you mess around with small stuff, you'll lose money, because Toby only has so many hours and she has to invest them with those who will pay serious shekels."

Max looked at Minnie. "Well, I guess we can give it a go."

"What else can we do?" asked his wife.

"Great," said the Oracle, returning to his favorite rock. "Now that we have that settled, what's for dessert?"

Minnie opened the basket. "We thought you might like a melon medley with rainbow sorbet."

"Ooooo!" said the Oracle. "I haven't had a good sorbet in decades!"

Minnie's Notes . . .

Ozzie the Oracle's Bedrock Questions—
with Answers for a Wizard Seller Market

1. Who are our customers?
   - New users who need expert assistance from the seller—often both before and after the sale—on an extended basis to deal with the complexities of technology and the purchase transaction
   - Specific customers include not only the financial decision maker but also line managers and users who have influence over the sale

2. Who are our competitors?
   - Established technology (camels, sledges, etc.), but also competitors offering their own configurations of our technology (i.e., Imum's Wheelbarrow).

3. Why do customers want what we are selling?
   - They want a performance gain, but they also want the technology to come from a seller who provides extended assurances of the desired results and personal attention to solving any problems associated with the technology's performance

4. What would make them prefer to buy from us?
   - We offer the best solution—and back it with the best support and service

5. Why might they prefer to buy from our competitors?
   - Established competitors offer proven, low-tech solutions
   - New competitors claim to offer superior results

6. What added values does our salesperson have to offer to make a sale?
   - A special blend of technical savvy so that the wizard can provide an expert solution customized to the buyer's individual needs, and "people skills" to be a team player managing a number of different relationships

14

Toby the Wizard was now in her glory.

As soon as Max and Minnie gave her the okay, Toby put together a plan on how to sell the Wheel and went to work.

The first thing Toby wanted to do was to build the image of Max's Wheel Company. She wanted the company to be seen as smart, progressive, and being on the cutting edge of technology. Which was all pretty much true, but most of the world did not know that yet.

A while back, Toby had attended one of the Pharaoh's gala dinner soirees. There she had been seated next to Phil of Phoenicia, also known as Phil the Phlack.

Long ago, a "phlack" was a person who, for a fee, would work to enhance your reputation by publicizing your accomplishments or your good deeds (or those of your company). Today, these people are known as "public-relations professionals."

Minnie's Notes . . .

The best way to generate sales leads in a wizard's market is to offer free information—via publicity, brochures, speaking engagements, and other means.

Anyway, Phil and Toby got to talking, and at the end of the dinner they exchanged cards.

Now, Toby sent for Phil and told him, "You know, I might have a project for you. Are you interested?"

"How big is your budget?"

"Ten thousand shekels."

"I'm interested," said Phil.

A week later, Phil the Phlack was having lunch with the editor of the *Ancient Science Journal*.

After a few goblets of Greek wine, Phil leaned across the table and said, "Listen, I think I might have something for you. How'd you like an exclusive inside story on how they're building the Great Pyramid?"

"Would I? You bet!"

"Not a problem," said Phil. "I'll set it up for you."

A couple of months later, the *Ancient Science Journal* ran a cover story:

AN ASJ EXCLUSIVE!
BREAKTHROUGH WHEEL TECHNOLOGY
PUTS GREAT PYRAMID
ON THE HORIZON!

Inside was a big article about the Great Pyramid, but it was written in such a way as to feature the Wheel. In fact, it had been written mostly by Phil the Phlack. Max and Minnie were quoted extensively. Plus, there were pictures and a long interview with Toby, "Wheel Wizard."

Soon, other stories of a similar nature began to appear in *Egyptian Age* and *Monument* magazine. Even the ultraconservative *Caravan Manager* ran a story on the Wheel—though with a negative twist, strongly hinting that the Wheel was unsafe.

Phil also arranged speaking engagements for Toby. She gave the keynote address at the Nile Contractors' Convention, and she conducted a half-day seminar in rotational mechanics hosted by the prestigious Camel Club.

The effect of this exposure was both powerful and quickly felt.

First and most obvious, Toby established the company and herself as the leading authority on the subject.

Second, after reading one of the articles or after hearing her give a talk, people began to approach her for advice. How might *they* apply the Wheel to their own businesses?

Indeed, by giving away free information about the Wheel, she made people realize how little they really knew about this powerful new technology. By offering a small amount of knowledge, she showed potential customers how much they needed her expertise.

Toby had scribes make copies of these stories. She could then distribute these to people with whom she wanted to meet. They were the perfect introduction—almost as good as a referral by the Pharaoh himself.

One evening at the Camel Club, Toby had just concluded the question-and-answer session following her speech, "Torque: Force of the Future."

She was basking in the polite applause of the audience when she noticed a rather distinguished man waiting for the chance to approach her.

Indeed, as the crowd began to break up, the man did approach. He extended his hand and said, "Very interesting talk you gave."

"Thank you."

"My name is Samuel Tonn. I'm vice president of product development at the Goliath Sledge Corporation."

"I've heard of you," said Toby. (In fact, she had been sending him letters and press clippings for months, hoping to arrange a meeting—to no avail up to now.)

"I think you make a convincing case that Wheels and sledges were made for each other. And your work at the Great Pyramid speaks for itself. I was wondering if you could meet with some of my people over at Goliath Sledge and discuss the possibility of adding Wheels to some of our products?"

"Why, of course, Sam. Let me give you my card."

15

Now, you might think that it would be a cinch at this point for Toby to win business from the Goliath Sledge Corporation. You might think that all Toby had to do was show up, have a meeting with Sam Tonn, close the sale, and bring home the order.

Nope, uh-uh, didn't work that way.

You see, Goliath Sledge was an established, large, rather convoluted organization. At Goliath Sledge, nobody did anything without getting at least a half dozen other people involved. No one there worked independently, and nobody could make a unilateral decision.

So it was very difficult for an outsider to sell much of anything at "the Sledge." And, according to many, it was impossible to sell the Sledge a new idea.

A case in point: Cassius the Closer had already been there. Several years earlier, the great salesman had got in to see old Joe Plank, the president and CEO of Goliath Sledge. Cassius had demonstrated the Wheel and had impressed the heck out of old Joe—but nothing had come of it. Cassius had even left behind a sample pair of Wheels. These were now gathering dust in a storage room over at Goliath Sledge's R&D lab.

Toby had heard this story, yet she was undaunted.

When Cassius the Closer made a sales presentation, it was, you might say, not unlike a wrestling match—one-on-one.

But Toby often handled sales presentations as if they were a team sport—that is, group-on-group.

The reason for the difference was efficiency. For Cassius, who was conducting a relatively simple sales transaction, the most efficient way to get the job done was to isolate the key decision maker and then go to work.

For Toby, who was trying to make a rather complex transaction in which there were a lot of issues to be sorted out, the most efficient way to do it was to get all of the customer's decision makers—and decision influencers—together in one place and then work with them as a group.

Unlike Cassius, she often did not work alone. For the presentation to Goliath Sledge, she put together a team that would match up against the people on the customer's side.

Knowing that Joe Goliath, the company president, would be in attendance, she brought along Max, the president of her company. (And she made sure that Max and Joe were seated near each other at the table.)

She also knew that Zach, Goliath's vice president of engineering, would be there. So Toby also brought one of Max's Wheel Company's new employees, Ruth the Designer.

By having a team assist her, Toby could get across the not-so-subtle message that her company offered leadership and depth, and that the customer could expect a lot of support through the course of its association with Max's Wheel Company.

Not only did she assemble a team, she put together a game plan—she and the others rehearsed the presentation so that each person would know what to say and when to say it during the meeting.

Toby let Max open with a brief background of the Wheel's development. Then she took over to talk about the Great Pyramid job, what a huge undertaking it had been, and how retrofitting Wheels to sledges had proven invaluable for moving the big stones. (And she made sure to include references to the technical support the Pyramid builders had received.)

Next, she turned it back to Max, who posed, and then answered, the question "What might Wheels mean to your business?"

This was a terrific, blue-sky, conceptual discussion of the power of Wheel technology and how it might change the world as they knew it.

> **Minnie's Notes . . .**
>
> A big part of a wizard's job in sales is to educate the customer.

But following this, upon a tap under the table from Toby, Ruth the Designer brought the presentation down to earth by describing how completely practical it would be to manufacture sledges with Wheels on them.

Then, at exactly the right moment, Toby stood up, went to the easel at the head of the table, and unveiled . . .

". . . possibly the next billion shekels in sales growth for Goliath Sledge: a Wheeled system that we call the Wagon."

Well, on the customer's side of the table, chins were stroked and glances were exchanged. They were impressed.

Yet, as always, despite the well-planned and professional manner of the presentation, there were customer objections—worries, doubts, and concerns. Indeed, Toby was expecting these and had even anticipated many of them.

"I'll grant you that this Wagon device you've proposed looks intriguing. But suppose one of these Wagons goes out of control on a hill or something. What if it starts rolling faster and faster? What if it kills someone? We could be sued!"

"Not according to our legal counsel," said Toby, "assuming you've done nothing negligent and have given the proper safety warnings. In any case, there is always the possibility of accidents, even with your conventional sledges. Clearly, the benefits of Wagons far outweigh the potential risks."

Then came the doubts about whether Max's Wheel Company really offered the best design solution.

"Okay, if we do decide to pursue the Wagon concept—not that I'm necessarily saying we should, mind you—are we sure that we really want *round* Wheels? What about octagonal Wheels?"

"Yes, there has been some research on octagonal—and even hexagonal—Wheels. But our testing clearly demonstrates that round Wheels are the way to go."

"What about this guy Imum, the one who invented the Wheelbarrow? Maybe we should talk to him before we go ahead with anything. Perhaps we don't need a Wagon with four Wheels—why, heck, we could just put one Wheel underneath right in the middle. Be a lot cheaper, wouldn't it?"

"Cheaper, yes, but far less stable. Research clearly shows that Imum's Wheelbarrow approach has some severe limitations. It's not a design we would recommend."

Then came the golden objection, the one that could be used to make the sale:

"Let's say we go ahead with the Wagon. How do we know there won't be problems with it? How do we know our customers will want to buy Wagons?"

Going into the presentation, Toby had known that it was highly unlikely that Goliath Sledge would immediately give the green flag to building Wagons. She would have happily accepted an uncon-ditional *yes*, but in lieu of that she was prepared to make an interim sale that could well lead to much bigger business later on.

"I think the prudent way to proceed," said Toby, "is to do a pi-lot project that will produce a Wagon prototype. We can field test the prototype, resolve any design flaws, and then show it to a group of your customers and collect data on their reactions. If the response is as favorable as we think it will be, you can proceed with large-scale manufacturing and we can ramp up our own pro-duction to supply you with Wheels."

This proved to be the perfect option. This way, conservative Goliath Sledge could commit without committing. And all it would cost, Toby informed them, was a million shekels—a mere bucket of sand from the desert in terms of the corporation's vast resources.

On the customer's side, there were nods all around.

"Let's go ahead with it," said Joe Goliath.

"Excellent," said Toby. "All I need is your signature on this let-ter of agreement in order for us to set the Wheels in motion, so to speak."

Once Toby had made the sale to the Sledge, she simply did everything else she'd done so expertly at the Great Pyramid.

She stayed in touch with the customer and kept them advised on the progress of the prototype.

She responded to all manner of special needs and requests, the silly as well as the legitimate.

She continued to educate everyone at the Sledge about the nature of Wheels.

And, overall, she managed every aspect of the project—not just the technical issues, but also the relationships with the cus-tomer.

Indeed, when necessary, in order to deal smoothly with the many diverse personalities and rivalries inside the Sledge, she even became a bit of a politician.

Before the year was out, despite any number of design changes,

Ozzie's Insights . . .

Top Characteristics of World Class Sales Wizards

- They are team players, and often leaders of teams that will implement a complete solution. They have the ability to work with—and around—the bureaucracy of the customer's organization so as to "get things done."
- Strong sense of responsibility for the consequences of the sale.
- In-depth personal understanding of the technical issues involved in the sale. Experts in their own right.
- Professional demeanor. Affluent, but not too flashy in personal appearance or lifestyle.
- Fast learners, able to assimilate not only the intricacies of what they are selling, but also the often-complex requirements of each new customer to whom they sell.
- They document performance so as to prove the benefit of the solution—and perhaps gain add-on sales.
- Focus on selling total systems—particularly a custom-designed total solution—not subassemblies or pieces and parts.
- Common liabilities: arrogance; tendency to overpromise benefits and underestimate the resources required for the solution.

the Wagon prototype was working—and it was a technical tour de force.

To show it off—and in large part to gather support within the organization—they rolled it from one end of the Sledge factory to the other, and wherever the Wagon appeared, employees in every department cheered and applauded.

"Looks good," said Zach of Engineering, after concluding his final inspection of the prototype Wagon. "But you need to field test it."

So they went to a field.

They were rolling the Wagon back and forth through the field, testing it, and of course Toby and Ruth were on hand because these were important tests. And then a great and nearly disastrous event took place.

The field that they had chosen for the testing, as it happened, was next to a granary.

A granary, back in ancient times, was a place where grain was stored between the harvest and whenever people needed it for food.

On this particular day, the grain had just been harvested from the fields and there were dozens of workers next to the granary thrashing the grain with flails.

See, back then, they would use a long, sticklike tool, called a flail to beat the wheat (or whatever they were thrashing) to crack the hulls and release the grain inside.

So the granary workers were thrashing, the Sledge engineers were testing, and Toby and Ruth were standing by awaiting the results—when suddenly the Wagon began to roll down a hill.

The Wagon just got away from everyone, and it was rolling faster and faster and faster, and no one could stop it.

"Look out!" Toby called to the granary workers.

"Run for your lives!" called Zach of Engineering.

Hearing these warnings, the granary workers parted like the Red Sea—and the Wagon, on its huge heavy stone Wheels, rolled right over the grain spread on the ground.

Finally, the Wagon, after rolling some distance, slowed to a stop.

"You see!" Zach of Engineering said to Toby. "Wheels are unsafe!"

"Now, now," said Toby. "At least no one got hurt. I'm sure if we put our heads together, we can come up with a solution."

"No, we're going to have to halt the testing immediately," said Zach. "We just can't risk these kinds of accidents."

Whereupon, he promptly departed for headquarters.

By now, the granary manager, Mr. Loaf, had come outside to see what all the commotion was about.

"I'm terribly sorry about your grain," Toby said to him, hoping to smooth things over. "Some of it seems to have been crushed, but we'll be happy to pay for any damages."

"Hey," said one of the workers, "look at this! Those big, heavy stone Wheels did the thrashing for us!"

At this, Mr. Loaf made a closer inspection. Indeed, the weight of the Wheel had easily cracked open the hulls, releasing the grain.

"Say, what is that thing?" asked Mr. Loaf, inquiring about the Wagon.

"Do you mind if we borrow it?" another of the workers asked.

"Go ahead," said Toby.

So the workers dropped their flails and took turns rolling the Wagon back and forth through the field, thrashing the grain in this new way with half the effort of before.

When Toby told this story to Max, she concluded by saying, "The only good thing that happened was that Mr. Loaf made me an offer right on the spot."

"For the Wagon?"

"No, just for the Wheels."

Toby went back to Goliath Sledge. But the word was out. The Wagon was unsafe: It was dangerous. It was technology run amok.

Despite everything Toby said, despite her use of logic and every persuasive argument she could muster, no manager at the Sledge was about to risk a personal reputation backing the Wagon.

Max's Wheel Company, of course, was paid for all work to date, and it was quite a substantial sum. Nevertheless, poor Toby took this as a personal failure.

"I should have anticipated the hill problem," she said. "When we went down hills on the Great Pyramid project, they always moved the elephants to the back. I should have known."

"Well, they should have known better than to test it on a hill in the first place," said Minnie. "Look, maybe we can figure out a solution on our own, then take what we've learned and approach another sledge maker. Don't forget, Goliath might be the biggest sledge maker in the world, but it's not the only one."

In fact, there were the others of the Big Four sledge makers: Empire Sledge, Babylon Sledge, and, over in the ancient city of Ur, a regional competitor with the unfortunate name of Sledges Ur Us.

> **Minnie's Notes . . .**
>
> One risk of the wizard's market: you might commit big resources to technology that might not, in the end, be accepted.

The word was that all of these had taken notice of the Wheel, and rumors had been circulating for some time that Imum had engaged a wizard of his own and was in talks with several of the Big Four to produce a commercial version of the Wheelbarrow. (The wildest of these suggested a radical redesign of the Wheelbarrow that included a mysterious *second* Wheel.)

Yet even as Toby prepared to approach these other manufacturers, Max was working on something completely different. One day, he asked Minnie and Toby into his office.

"Forget the Wagon," he told them.

"What? How can we do that after all the work we've put in!" cried Toby.

Max unfurled some drawings onto a table and said, "Check *this* out."

Minnie examined the drawings, but couldn't comprehend what they depicted.

"It looks like two Wheels," said Toby, "one set perpendicularly on top of the other."

"Yes," said Max, "that's exactly right. It's the Millstone."

"The Millstone?"

"Well, actually the Millstone System. See, after that granary episode, I got to thinking: Why not use the weight and durability of the stone Wheel to its greatest advantage? Hence, the Millstone. It's made of two heavy stone Wheels, not unlike the kind we already make. One is horizontal, flat on its side, and the other is upright, on top of the first."

"What's it do?" asked Minnie.

"A Millstone will mill grain!" said Max. "See, the top Wheel is connected to the Axle of the first Wheel on the bottom by a turnstile type of device. And it rolls 'round and 'round the face of the bottom Wheel."

He then explained how workers would throw unshucked wheat onto the flat face of the Wheel on the bottom. They would then push the second Wheel around the circumference of the first, thereby crushing the hulls.

"And presto!" said Max. "Shucked grain without all that flailing around."

"Brilliant," said Toby.

"Thank you," said Max. "But here is the really big question: Do you think can sell these things?"

Toby thought about it for a few minutes, then said, "You just watch me."

And sell them she did.

Indeed, with the Millstone, Toby found exactly what she was born to sell.

For its day, it was a high-tech system. Nothing else quite like it had entered the market.

Each sale was complex—because every Millstone System had to be matched to each granary's special needs.

The buyers and users of Millstones were novices; they needed an expert like Toby to help guide them. Should Millstones be beveled and grooved, or just beveled, or flat? The Millstones themselves were custom fitted, and different stones worked better for different types of grain. You needed a wizard to help sort out what was best for your situation.

Just like at the Great Pyramid, there was a multitude of issues, like training the workers and doing the maintenance, that had to be bundled into the total price, because the customers were buying a total solution from a single source.

But this also meant that Max and Minnie could charge a premium. In fact, if granary customers wanted Millstones, they had little choice except to buy the whole kit and pay the price for it. Max and Minnie were making thirty to fifty percent net income on each Millstone System Toby sold.

Meanwhile, by hiring apprentice wizards and training them, Toby was able to keep selling regular stone Wheels for retrofitting to all the remaining sledges out there in the ancient world—a dwindling but still significant market, and a very profitable one, so long as Toby's wizards focused on the larger fleets of sledges.

In short, Max and Minnie were raking it in. Whereas the Great Pyramid had brought in a million shekels in revenue, quite soon the company was making a million shekels in profit. With that much money coming in every year, why worry?

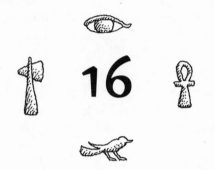

16

Because, suddenly, everything was different.

Toby the Wizard came back from a business trip, having won yet another contract for a Millstone System, and in going through her mail found the latest issue of *Wheel Age* magazine.

You should bear in mind that *Wheel Age* was a fairly new publication, just a year old, and the cover of its very first issue had highlighted a feature story with Toby's byline (though the story had, in fact, been written by Phil the Phlack) with the title "Big? Small? Wide? Thin? Which Stone Wheels Are the Right Retrofit for *Your* Sledge?"

Toby, of course, had immediately signed up for a lifetime subscription. But *now*, in big gaudy letters splashed across the cover, the magazine proclaimed:

THE WOODIES ARE HERE!
THE WOODIES ARE HERE!
WOODEN WHEELS COME OF AGE!!

The entire issue was filled with story after story on wheels made of wood. And, yes, the magazine no longer capitalized *wheel*. Because the word *wheel* no longer applied to a single, proprietary product.

In this special issue were charts comparing features and tables of lab-test data. There was a roundup article describing all of the different wooden wheels that were now available. There was a tear-out "Upgrade Guide" on swapping wooden wheels for the old stone Wheels. Most offensive to Toby was the editorial headlined with the question STONE WHEELS: ARE THEY ANCIENT HISTORY?

Indeed, the editorial, after several paragraphs that purported to weigh the evidence, concluded that stone Wheels would soon be a thing of the past—except in limited applications like Millstones.

"Why bother with heavy, breakable, expensive stone Wheels," wrote the editor, "when light, strong, repairable, and affordable wooden wheels are fast becoming the standard?"

Finally, on the back cover, Toby found a big, colorful gatefold advertisement from none other than the Imum Wheel Company, "Makers of the Original Woody Wheel!"

Toby ran to show the magazine to Max.

"What are we going to do?" she asked him. "I don't think we even have a wooden wheel on the drawing board, do we?"

"Aw, don't worry about it," said Max, tossing the magazine into the wastebasket. "These wooden wheels, they'll never hold up over time. They're just a passing fad."

◆   ◆   ◆

But the "fad" failed to pass.

Instead, a head-spinning multitude of changes began to occur with alarming rapidity. Out of the blue, Goliath Sledge declared bankruptcy. *Nobody* was buying sledges anymore. In a fairly short time, sales arced downward from millions to zero, and Goliath fell on its face.

The cause of Goliath's demise? David's Ox Cart Company, an upstart enterprise that had worked with Imum to develop a radical new two-wheeled variant of the Wheelbarrow.

Everybody nowadays was buying ox carts, Wheelbarrows—and, soon, *wagons* as well. A former Goliath executive took the wagon concept that Max and Toby had pioneered, commercialized it, and started the Hercules Wagon Company. Furthermore, not every sledge manufacturer was as slow on the uptake as Goliath. Soon, even the most conservative of sledge makers were bringing out something with wheels.

Now, they varied in design. Some had three wheels, some had six, and one even had a dozen. And the wheels were different diameters, sometimes huge, sometimes tiny. But all the wheels had one thing in common: they were all made of wood. And almost all of those wheels came from Imum.

"That bum!" thundered Max.

"Who?" asked his wife.

"*Imum the bum!*" Max stormed. "First he steals my idea! Now he makes out like a bandit! Look at this . . ."

He showed Minnie the inspiration for his ire: the new copy of *Ancient TIME* magazine. On the cover was the grinning face of Imum. He had been named Entrepreneur of the Year!

The story that announced the award gushed over Imum's brilliance as an inventor.

"A mechanical genius with a head for business!" wrote the story's writer.

There was nary a mention of Max or Minnie or the original Wheel.

"Here we are, the company that helped build the Great Pyramid! The company that gave the world the Millstone! But who do they remember? The inventor of the Wheelbarrow!"

His wife sighed. "All this ranting and raving isn't going to help, Max. We've got to accept reality: wooden wheels are the wave of the future."

"Not in gristmills!" Max rumbled. "To make flour, you need a Mill*stone*, not a Mill*wood*!"

"Yes, but, Max, think of it: You could take all the Millstone sales for the next five years, and the total wouldn't add up to the market just for ox cart wheels for one year alone. Then you've got your wagons . . . and that new thing they're supposed to be developing for the military, the chariot, and—"

"Yeah, yeah, I hear you."

"Good," said his wife. "I'm glad you're finally listening. Because we're not making money the way we used to. Toby hasn't sold *any* wheels for sledge retrofits in more than six months. Everybody who owns a sledge is chopping it up for firewood. It's *cheaper* just to buy a new wagon than it is to put wheels on an old sledge.

"Max, if you insist, we can stick with Millstones. We've got a market there worth a few million shekels. But the market for wooden wheels is going to be worth *hundreds* of millions—and it's all going to go to Imum if we don't act now. His wheels are fast becoming the standard. If we don't do something quick, he's going to be impossible to beat."

Max fumed and grumbled, but he knew she was right. He silently paced the floor for several minutes. Finally, he stopped and said, "Okay, fine. If Imum can go one better on my idea, I can go one better on his."

◆   ◆   ◆

Max set to work. He and Toby and the company engineers worked quickly but brilliantly. Before long, they had created a wooden wheel that, as they put it, "was worthy of the Max's Wheel Company name."

Indeed, tests soon revealed that it was not only as good as a Woody—it was better.

It had spokes.

This meant it was lighter than, but just as strong and durable as, a Woody Wheel, which was solid.

Max's new "Spoked Wheels" were a breakthrough in design. They were also slightly cheaper to manufacture than Woody Wheels.

And they looked cool, too.

"I just know these Spoked Wheels are going to be an instant hit," claimed Max.

Unfortunately, he still had a lot to learn about sales.

With these hot, new Spoked Wheels to sell, Minnie and Toby decided to go after the wagon and ox cart makers, who were then the biggest buyers of wheels in the known world.

Before long, using credentials such as those garnered on the Great Pyramid project, Toby was able to secure an appointment with none other than the President of the Atlas Wagon Company, the "new leader in heavy-duty transport," as its ads claimed.

But her first meeting did not go as she had planned. Halfway into her presentation, as she was talking about Max's Wheel Company's many capabilities, the President interrupted her.

"This is all very impressive," he said, "but I take it you're here to sell wheels?"

"Well . . . yes."

"Then you should be talking to our Wheel Department."

"Oh. You have a Wheel Department?"

"That's right. Our Wheel Department handles everything to

do with the wheels that go on our wagons. If you'll just follow me, I'll take you down there and introduce you to the people you need to know."

"That would be terrific," said Toby.

A few minutes later, Toby found herself making her presentation to Cyrus, the Manager of Wheel Specification, and Bibi, Atlas's Manager of Wheel Procurement.

Because of the introduction by the President, they made time for Toby and listened respectfully—but rather coolly.

"To tell you the truth," Cyrus told Toby, "your Spoked Wheels do look rather promising. But they're not what we'll be needing this year."

"May I ask why not?"

Cyrus and Bibi exchanged glances. Then Bibi explained in a somewhat condescending tone, "You see, we have to work at least a year in advance on this kind of a change."

"That's right," said Cyrus. "Our designs for this model year have already been approved and finalized."

"Oh, but that's no problem," said Toby. "I can bring in a team of engineers and we can work with you to modify those designs."

"No, I'm sorry, that's just not how we do things here at the Atlas Wagon Company," said Cyrus.

"However, since you could be a vendor we might like to do business with at some point," said Bibi, "I can give you the specifications for wheels we plan to buy over the next six to twelve months, and you can work up a quote on price and delivery terms."

"Well, ah, all right."

"By the way, what kind of color options can you offer?"

"Color . . . options?"

"Yes. We find, for instance, that red is a very popular color with wagon buyers this year, and naturally we'd like the wheels to match."

"Whatever color you need, I'm sure we can handle it," Toby answered in a less-than-enthusiastic tone.

Clearly this was not like selling Millstones or even the Wheels for the Pyramids. In those situations, the customers had depended on her technical knowledge. They had consulted her. They had sought cutting-edge solutions from her. Here, it was all cut and dried. They were telling her what kind of wheels they would allow her to supply.

"It's as if they think they know as much about wheels as I do," she later complained to Minnie. "I mean, I *am* a licensed wizard, and yet they don't even want to hear my opinions on their designs!"

"Well, they are the customer," Minnie reminded her. "And we need their business."

"Okay, I'll keep trying," said Toby.

Yet when she delivered the price quote that they had asked for, everything fell apart. The "quote" was more like a proposal—the sort of thing her Millstone clients so much appreciated—but Cyrus and Bibi hardly knew what to make of it.

"And these prices!" exclaimed Bibi. "These are way out of line. You're a good thirty to forty percent higher than our main supplier."

"Oh, but you have to realize that engineering support and project management are included in those prices," said Toby.

"What? We don't need those things," said Cyrus. "Look, what we want are standard solid wheels, with good quality and the right options, delivered on time every time—and at a competitive price."

"I'm sorry," said Bibi, "but I think we'll stay with the vendor we have now."

"Might I ask who that is?"

Somewhat reluctantly, Bibi told her. "We deal with Imum Wheel Company."

Thereafter, it got worse.

At the Hercules Wagon Company, the counterparts of Cyrus and Bibi asked Toby about restocking programs.

"Restocking programs?" She'd never heard of such things.

"Yes, we're interested in vendors who will deliver inventories on a just-in-time basis."

At David's Ox Cart Company, they would hardly give Toby the time of day.

"We have a long-term contract with Imum for all the wheels we need," they told her.

Finally, Toby had to be honest with herself—and with Max and Minnie.

"I hate to say this," she said to them, "but this kind of selling just doesn't interest me. It is so boring. And they treat me like . . . like a peddler!"

Max turned to Minnie, and Minnie said, "Well, we don't know what else to tell you. This market is going to be very important, and we need to gain a foothold in it."

"Please," said Toby, "I'm begging you. Put me back selling Millstone Systems. I feel needed there, and with Millstones every system is different. At least I'm not selling the same darn wheel day in and day out."

"But, Toby—"

"If you can't put me back in Millstones, I'm going to have to resign," she said.

"All right, hold on," said Max. "Let's not be hasty."

Even though Toby had bombed in the wagon market, she was still very talented, and Max and Minnie did not want to lose her.

"Give us some time to think this over," said Minnie, "and we'll talk again in a few days."

Part Three

EVERYBODY
WANTS
WHEELS!

17

F_{ew} entrepreneurs in the history of business were more frustrated than Max was at this point in time.

After years and years of hard work, the wheel had become an overnight success. And now that everybody wanted wheels, everybody's *brother* wanted into the wheel market.

Dozens—even hundreds—of new, little companies were springing up all over the place, their owners expecting to stake out some piece of the wheel phenomenon. Some would actually make wheels. Some would make the wagons, ox carts, and wheelbarrows that used the wheels. Others wanted to be the dealers selling those products. Still more opened shops to service and maintain these wheels and wagons and everything else wheel-related that everybody was buying.

And why? Because it was common knowledge that you could make serious shekels in the wheel business.

Yet, even though the wheel business was booming all around

them, Max's Wheel Company, pioneers of the original concept, seemed headed for bust.

"Well, no, not quite," Minnie reminded her husband. "Don't forget, we're still number one in Millstones."

"But that's not where the action is!" Max complained.

After he pacing the living room a while, he took out his wallet to see how many shekels he had with him.

"Come on," he told his wife. "We're going to the market to buy whatever we need to make the best meal we can think of."

The next day, having followed the narrow path along the river, up the winding canyon, into the arid mountains populated only by bugs and snakes, Max and Minnie arrived once again at the mouth of the dark and forbidding cave.

Once inside, Max took sticks from the pile and got a fire going. Minnie filled a big black kettle with water and put this on the fire to boil. Next to it, she set up the chafing dish and loaded that with butter. Then Max skewered a generous cut of filet mignon and set it over the flames to broil.

The scent of the butter and the aroma of the steak wafted back into the nether parts of the cave, and soon, like magic, Ozzie the Oracle appeared.

"Mmm-mmm! Smells good! What, pray tell, is the burnt offering *du jour*?" asked the Oracle.

"Surf and turf."

"One of my favorites!" His eyes lit up, and he readily produced a lobster bib from a hidden pocket inside his robes. But as he was tying on the bib, his expression changed. "To bring me a meal like this, you must have a doozy of a problem."

"Right, as always," said Max.

And as the Oracle devoured the sumptuous offering with gusto, Max and Minnie explained their situation.

◆   ◆   ◆

"Well," said the Oracle, swirling the last chunk of lobster in the last of the melted butter, "it's not hopeless."

"But there's not a lot of cause for optimism, either," said Max. "Is that what you mean?"

"What it comes down to is that you have a big strategic decision to make," said the Oracle. "Either you can follow the technology . . . or you can follow the market."

"Uh-huh. But . . . what do you mean?"

"Let's say you take the first choice. You choose to be a technology company. In that case, you're going to have to reinvent the Wheel."

"Reinvent the Wheel? Why?"

"By that, I mean your future growth will be based on your ability to create new advances in technology. You'll be on a path that takes you into territories of undiscovered knowledge. The role of your company is to sell what you learn—and what you can make useful—through products and services. Now, if you make this choice, you won't have to change very much in terms of your market strategy and your company's culture. Yours is already a technology company."

"So . . . we'd keep on selling Millstones or what?" asked Minnie.

"Millstones, advanced Millstones, and whatever other new, high-tech products you can create from your research and development."

"Oh, you mean like when I wake up in the middle of the night with a new brilliant idea," said Max.

The Oracle rolled his eyes. "Anyway, let's say you keep on developing and selling new technology. You could do quite well. You'd keep on using salespeople like Toby—wizards and other technical experts who also know how to sell. Or you might again retain the services of a closer like Cassius if you're selling the next wave of high-end, high-tech products that are sold 'as is' with no extensive support and no custom alterations, just a wham-bam-thank-you kind of a sale."

"Wait a minute. If we do this, will the company be profitable?" asked Max.

"It can be. Very profitable, in fact. But there are some caveats. Like you'll have to accept that your company will probably never be huge. It'll probably never be a household name. The kind of business you'll be doing will tend to be project work—do the job and move on—rather than steady, continuing business. And as you keep learning, keep developing, you'll also forever have to keep finding *new* customers."

"I'm not sure I like that part of it," said Max.

"Well, technology is only new to so many people for so long. Then it becomes familiar, and they don't need a Cassius to convince them to take the plunge or a Toby to teach them how to use it. You see, as a technology ages and matures, it becomes familiar to the people who buy it and use it. As the number of these experienced customers increases, they begin to outnumber the newbies—"

"Newbies?"

"The novices. The inexperienced customers. See, until recently, most of those who were buying wheel products had no prior experience with them. That's what is now changing. An ever-increasing segment of the world has tried the wheel and found it to be of benefit. The market of *experienced* users is getting larger and larger. Coincidentally, that's why you're seeing so many competitors jump into the fray right now, because the market is expanding so dramatically.

"Which brings me to your other option: You can follow the market. You can sell standardized wheels to a growing market of experienced customers."

"All right, if we do 'follow the market,' " said Max, "that means what?"

"It means you have to cater to this growing number of customers who have bought and used wheels in the past, as opposed to the relatively shrinking number of potential buyers who still don't know a wheel from a dinner plate.

"But, Max, if you follow this path and take your company into the territory of the growing market, you're going to have to adopt a whole new marketing plan and a very different style of selling."

"Why is that?"

"A number of reasons. As a technology grows in popularity, it also tends to become standardized. If you try to introduce a non-standard product, or sometimes even just a slightly different version of that product, very often the experienced customer will hesitate—or even balk."

"Is that what's happening with our Spoked Wheels?"

"To a degree, yes," said the Oracle. "Now, I'm not saying you shouldn't work hard to improve the wheel. But you're going to have to be a bit patient, and your improvements from here on can't be too radical. What you've got to do, year after year, is offer a product that's just *a little bit* better, *a little bit* more feature-rich—and a little bit lower in cost—than last year's product.

"Veteran customers pretty much know what they want—or at least they know what they value. They don't need your salesperson telling them what they should have. That's not to say they don't need someone to help them through the sale. They often do. And they need someone to help them when they have a problem."

"Okay," said Minnie, "but why does that mean a whole new selling style?"

"Think about it. Put yourself in the place of, say, Atlas Wagon," said the Oracle. "If you've got your own internal experts on staff—a whole Wheel Department—would *you* want some arrogant wizard telling you what you needed, trying to complicate your life with custom designs, with advanced technology you don't want or might not need?"

"No, I guess not."

"Ah, but keep in mind, Atlas Wagon isn't buying wheels by the dozen. They're buying wheels by the thousands. By the tens of thousands. That kind of sale isn't simple. You've got to think about where you're going to put these ten thousand wheels when they show up. You've got to think about what happens to your factory if a delivery *doesn't* show up. What if some of those wheels aren't really round? What if they show up and they're *pink* instead of red? So, tell me, if you're Atlas Wagon, what kind of things are you going to be looking for in a supplier?"

"Well . . . I guess I'd be looking for someone reliable."

"Right."

"Someone who would pay close attention to details."

"You bet."

"Someone who would make darn sure nothing ever got screwed up," said Minnie.

"Yes, but let's say that despite best efforts, some kind of problem *did* come up?"

"I'd want a salesperson who would go to bat for me. Someone who would get things straightened out—and quick."

"Yep."

"Someone I could trust," added Max.

"Bingo!"

"Someone who would treat me special. Someone who would build a good relationship with me and my company. Someone who cared."

"Absolutely."

"And, of course, someone who would work to get me the best possible price," said Minnie.

"You two go to the head of the class!" shouted the Oracle.

"Yeah, but where are we going to find someone like that?"

The Oracle shrugged. "Beats me."

18

Max and Minnie left the cave and came on down the mountain, talking the whole time about which path they and the company should follow.

Should they become what the biggest part of the market wanted?

Or should they keep inventing things that most of the market could not yet even imagine?

But even as they came trudging back into town, they could not decide.

"I guess I'm leaning toward the path of technology," said Max. "After all, that's what we know. We're just going to have to keep coming up with ever more brilliant inventions."

"But, Max, that's just it! Who's to say we're going to be able to keep inventing the Wheels and the Millstones of technology? How many more of those are you going to be blessed with?"

Max shrugged. Who could say?

"Besides," Minnie went on, "we already *have* great products. Why should we just give up the market for those to other companies?"

Home at last, Max found himself in a funk and began to pace the living room.

To change the subject a bit, his wife said, "There's a message here from Ben the Builder. He must have come by while we were gone."

"Yeah? What's it say?"

"Just that the Gladiators are back in town and . . . oh, look!" she said, unrolling the message all the way. "Ben's given us a couple of tickets for tonight's game!"

"That was nice of him," Max admitted. "You know, he's always doing that kind of thing. Hey, let's take him up on it. Maybe we can forget about business for a few hours."

"All right," said Minnie, "After all, there's nothing like a little senseless violence and mayhem to make you get your mind off your own problems."

They indeed went to the stadium that evening—it was a classic twi-night doubleheader, with the Assyrians battling the Hittites—and there was Ben the Builder.

He greeted Max and Minnie with a big smile and a warm handshake, and said, "Hey, glad you could make it!"

"Gee, these are great seats, Ben," said Minnie.

"Yeah, we'll be able to see all the action from here," said Max. "Wow, look at the size of those Hittites!"

"Yeah, should be a good one tonight. Help yourselves to the figs and camel fritters," Ben told them. "Oh, and let me introduce you to my good friends. Max, Minnie . . . I'd like you to meet Bibi and her colleague, Cyrus."

"How do you do," said Max, extending his hand. "Your names are familiar. Have we met before?"

"I don't think so," said Cyrus. "But perhaps we met through business. Bibi and I both work for Atlas Wagon."

"I see!" said Max.

"Very pleased to meet you!" said Minnie. "Tell me, how do you two know Ben?"

"Oh, we've been doing business with Ben for ages," said Bibi.

"He supplies all our camel needs," said Cyrus. "There's nobody we trust more than Ben."

Max and Minnie exchanged a glance, both thinking the same thought.

At evening's end, after Cyrus and Bibi had gone, Max and Minnie hung around a while.

"Hey, Ben, that was a heck of a match," said Max.

"Yeah, I thought the Assyrians might be able to hold out, but those Hittites were just way too tough."

"We had a great time," said Minnie. "Thanks for inviting us."

"Say, ah, Ben . . . do you have a few minutes to talk?"

"Sure!" said the salesman. "For you, I've got all the time in the world."

"Ben, Minnie and I had a few words together in private between the games and, ah . . . what would you think about coming to work for us?"

So they talked and soon they were shaking hands on a deal. Ben the Builder would come to work for Max's Wheel Company. It turned out that the camel dealership for whom Ben worked had not been

Minnie's Notes . . .

From first contact to closing the sale, a wizard works on a six-to-nine-month time frame. For a builder, the time frame is much longer—a couple of years or more. That's why World Class builders try to develop useful contacts long before they are needed.

treating him—or his customers—all that well, and Ben had been biding his time until the right opportunity came along.

Besides, Ben had always thought highly of the wheel's potential. It was simply a question of waiting until the market had matured enough to be ripe for his brand of selling.

The next day, they called Toby into the office for a talk.

"We have important news to tell you," said Max. "We're putting you back in Millstones."

"Yes," said Minnie, "but we're giving you a promotion. We're going to make you a vice president. You'll be running our new division: Advanced Wheel Systems."

"You'll be in charge of Millstones, and everything else that involves leading technology and a design tailored to a specific customer's requirements," said Max.

Toby was thrilled. This was exactly what she wanted.

"But what about the Spoked Wheel?" she asked. "It's a great product. Are you just going to forget about it?"

"No," said Max. "Not at all."

Ben the Builder went to work.

He went right over to Atlas Wagon, smiled, cracked a few jokes, slapped a few backs, gave them a price, and walked out with a million-shekel order. Right?

Wrong.

The wheel-supply contract for Atlas Wagon had already been awarded. Imum had the business.

Knowing Cyrus and Bibi on a personal basis merely got Ben the Builder through the gate and into their offices. It got him a friendly reception. It enabled him to take half an hour of their precious time to make his sales presentation—after which, Cyrus told him quite sincerely, "Great, Ben. We'll definitely keep you in mind."

"Fair enough," said Ben.

He left them some Max's Wheel Company product brochures and some cute little Spoked Wheel key chains, told them the one about the flatulent camel, left them chuckling, and waved good-bye.

"Patience," Ben reminded himself as his sandals touched the hot, dusty street. "I have to be patient."

But patience for Ben the Builder did not mean sitting around and twiddling his thumbs. Patience meant action.

Minnie's Notes . . .

Another term for the builder style is "relationship selling." However, having a <u>relationship</u> means more than just being "pals" with the customer. It means building a strong <u>working</u> relationship over an extended period of time.

19

Whenever Ben the Builder was thinking about bringing in new business, he began with three questions:

- First, who are the best customers I could have?
- Second, how do I get their attention?
- And, third, what are the best ways for them to get to know me?

Now, the very *best* customers were what we would call today "original equipment manufacturers"—the wagon builders, like Atlas, as well as the cart and chariot makers.

The reason they were the best customers to have was simple: each of them bought a lot of wheels. Plus, they were fairly large businesses that were growing ever larger—meaning that they had the resources to pay large invoices.

But there was another group of wheel buyers: the multitude of little companies that made up the rapidly expanding network of service and parts suppliers.

These were the folks who fixed your wagon—or your cart or your chariot, as the case may be. And they sold everything from pony harnesses to hubcaps. (Yes, there were hubcaps back then.) They were what we would call the "aftermarket." Of course, when wagon owners came in with wheels that were broken or worn out, they also sold replacements.

So while Ben was courting the big wagon makers and waiting for the right opportunity, he also began seeking out the best of the wagon fixers and replacement parts suppliers.

The trouble was that he didn't know any of them when he started. Or, as Ben himself wryly put it, "They don't know what a wonderful guy I am."

Well, from experience, Ben knew that there were a couple of good ways to handle that problem.

Minnie's Notes . . .

Builders, unlike closers and even wizards, often hate to make "cold calls"—that is, pay sales calls to total strangers.

One excellent, time-tested way was to join the same clubs, civic groups, and trade associations that your potential customers belonged to.

So Ben went right out and joined the WFA (Wagon Fixers Association), as well as the OCD (Ox Cart Dealers) and the HRCM (Hot Rod Chariot Modifiers).

But a second, very effective, way for getting to know future customers—which is to say, for generating leads—was to offer something for free.

Whereas Toby would give away free information—by speaking at meetings and publishing articles in professional journals—Ben's approach was to give away a free service.

Why? Well, in this market, most customers were fairly familiar with wheels by now. Hence, they didn't really want or need a lot of in-depth technical information.

And by giving away a service, Ben could prove one of his major strengths as a salesman: the ability to deliver service tailored to an individual customer's needs.

Therefore, Ben invented Wheel Safety Week.

Whenever Ben found someone who had just opened shop as a wagon fixer, he would write a letter that would go something like this:

> Dear Mr. Sanji:
>
> It has come to my attention that you have just entered the wagon-fixing business. Well, on behalf of Max's Wheel Company, I'd like to say congratulations! Welcome to a proud and rapidly growing profession. We wish you years of prosperity and success.
>
> To help get your young business off to a great start, I'd like to introduce you and your customers to Wheel Safety Week. It's a free service, and it's designed to bring people into your shop for a very important reason: safety.
>
> These days, with ever-increasing multitudes of wagons, ox carts, and chariots jamming our streets, everyone is concerned about safety—and no other single component is more vital to safety than a quality wheel. So in the interest of that most important issue, and to help everybody get better acquainted, we were hoping you would participate in Wheel Safety Week.
>
> Basically, it works like this: throughout a week of your choosing, every customer who drives a wagon, ox cart, or chariot to your shop gets Max's free, six-point Wheel Safety

Check. We will supply at no cost to you promotional materials, plus a trained technician and the required special tools to test for (1) wheel warp, (2) axle wear, (3) alignment, (4) camber, (5) cracking, and (6) squeaking, this last being a known contributor to drivers' insanity and the curse of Road Rage.

Wheel Safety Week is a great way for you to meet new customers in your neighborhood and, for those who need them, to sell new, quality wheels that improve both handling and confidence. In the next few days, I will dispatch one of my marathon messengers to run by and arrange an appointment so that I might drop by to go over the details with you—and to welcome you personally to what promises to be a great business for all of us.

> Sincerely,
> Ben the Builder
> Max's Wheel Company

With a letter of slightly different wording, Ben used the same idea to approach established wagon fixers—although he knew that the better opportunities were with those just entering the business who had not yet formed firm associations with any particular wheel manufacturer.

No matter what, Wheel Safety Week turned out to be a big hit. Everybody loved it. And the reason was that everybody benefited, often in several different ways.

First, the wagon drivers and owners were unburdened of their worries. In those days, it was not uncommon for wheels to fall apart, or come off the wagon, or fail in some way—and people had legitimate fears.

So the promotion answered a real need and was a true service, Ben knew, which was very important in order for something like this to work.

But, second, the wagon fixers got the chance to see lots of new faces come into their repair shops—and at a very low cost out of their own pockets. They got the goodwill and the credit for providing a public benefit. And they also sold lots of wheels—as well as axles, grease, and accessories.

There were plenty of benefits for Max's Wheel Company, too. During the promotion, everybody who stopped in, whether they needed replacement wheels or not, was offered product literature on Max's New, Improved Spoked Wheels. In fact, the company even sold some spoked wheels this way.

Now, statistically, Ben and his assistants found that about four out of every five wagons, carts, and chariots that came in during the week were okay. They didn't need new wheels. Which was fine with Ben. (Indeed, by supplying the technician who did the safety check, Ben made sure the event stayed honest, that there would be no bad press later because some grandmother got bilked by an unscrupulous wagon fixer for a new set of wheels on her ox-cart when she didn't really need them.)

The flip side of the coin was that one out of five wagons, or about twenty percent, *did* need to have a wheel or three or four replaced. And nine times out of ten, the replacements were Max's wheels.

In fact, Wheel Safety Week actually turned a slim to modest profit, even though there were real costs involved for the technicians' time, the signage, the ads, and so on.

"But to tell you the truth," Ben later told Minnie, "even if we just broke even, it would still be worth doing."

"Why is that?"

"Because everybody got to know each other. I got to know the wagon fixers over an extended pe-

Minnie's Notes . . .

Interestingly, builders do not give great service to all customers. They deliver great service to their best customers. Everyone else gets acceptable service. It's simply a matter of limited time and resources. Builders can't afford to develop an in-depth, personal relationship with everybody.

riod of time, and, in a way, that shows I'm on their side. It's like they almost owe me a favor now. And when I call on them next time, they're going to remember who I am. If I give them a competitive price, they're going to buy from me. Heck, some of them aren't even going to question the price; they'll just place the order.

"Here's something just as important, too: I made sure I hung around at each event, and I got to see up close how each wagon fixer operates. I know the ones that are well managed. I have a pretty good idea of the ones that are probably going to grow their businesses and make it over the long haul.

"You see, I can't spend equal time on every wagon fixer. There just aren't enough hours in the day. So I have no choice but to play favorites. And now I've got 'em picked out."

Well, Ben the Builder conducted Wheel Safety Weeks all over the ancient world (wherever reasonably practical), and they were so popular that any number of the wagon fixers and their customers asked Ben that Max's Wheel Company sponsor it again sometime.

Meanwhile, as all this was going on, Ben had certainly not forgotten about those good folks over at Atlas Wagon.

Even though they were not really customers, Ben still called on them any time he could find some reason—or, barring that, some fairly plausible excuse—to make contact.

Whenever the Gladiators were in town, naturally, Ben offered tickets to Cyrus and Bibi. And he read every issue of *Wagon Week* and other trade publications from cover

Minnie's Notes . . .

A key to gaining new customers in the builder's market is to capitalize on opportunity—oftentimes created when a competitor makes a mistake. Though builders operate differently from closers, they do have to have excellent closing skills, so as not to waste the opportunity when it presents itself.

to cover looking for stories that might be of interest to them—so that he could talk knowledgeably when he took them to lunch, and sometimes so that he could thoughtfully drop off a copy of the story next time he was in the neighborhood.

"You sure are investing a lot of time and money in Atlas," Minnie once commented—somewhat skeptically—as she scrutinized his expense report. "When is it ever going to pay off?"

"Minnie, I honestly don't know. But I do know this: If you treat them like a customer, eventually they'll become one."

"Yes, but when?"

"When Imum slips up. Someday, my counterpart at Imum is going to submit an invoice that's just a little too high. Or she's going to forget to pay attention to some detail—something that seems minor to her, but is major to them. Or she's going to start taking them for granted in some other way. Whatever it is, on that day, they're going to think of me, and I'm going to be there for them."

20

It was late one afternoon. Ben the Builder had just gotten back from a road trip, and he was tired. All he wanted to do was go home, have dinner, and relax. He was on his way out the door when a dusty, out-of-breath messenger came running in.

"Are you . . . are you Ben the Builder?" panted the runner.

"Yes."

"I'm glad I caught you. I have a message from Atlas Wagons. Cyrus would like to see you as soon as possible."

"You mean now?"

The messenger suddenly seemed confused. "Well . . . I suppose first thing in the morning would be all right. He said there was some kind of a problem and he needs to see you."

Ben thought about his schedule for the next day, and even without consulting his calendar, he knew it was full.

"Was he still in his office when you left?" Ben asked.

"Yes, both he and Bibi were going to wait until I returned with news of whether or not I'd reached you."

Ben nodded slowly. Tired though he was, a surge of energy filled him. "Well, you go on home. I'll go see them right now."

"Are you sure?"

"No problem."

As the messenger trotted off, Ben jumped into his chariot, which was parked at the curb, took the reins, and with a crack of the whip, went charging off.

When Ben got to Atlas Wagons, he walked in to find Cyrus dark with anger, while Bibi was pale with worry. One look at Ben, though, and their faces changed.

"I came as soon as I got word," said Ben. "Is there some kind of problem?"

Without answering, Cyrus handed to Ben a copy of the latest *Wagon Week*, open to the page with the news story announcing that the Hercules Wagon Company had been awarded a huge contract for 10,000 wagons being bought by the people of Babel for use in constructing a big tower.

Ben had already read the story and deliberately not sent it to Atlas, as he often did with news that affected them, because he suspected that they had probably bid on the contract and lost. In fact, he had made some discreet inquiries at Atlas Wagon, only to find out that Imum, its regular wheel supplier, had already been issued the purchase order for the 40,000 wheels that would be required.

"Yes, I've seen it."

"Well, now read this!" said Cyrus, handing Ben a letter written on Imum's stationery.

> Dear Valued Customer:
>   Due to recent unusually strong demand for wheel products, your standing order for 1,200 wheels per week may be delayed

by as much two to four weeks. We hope this does not inconvenience you. We are working around the clock to serve all of
our customers. Please bear with us during this busy period. If
there is anything further we can do for you, please don't hesitate to send a messenger. Thank you.

> Sincerely,
> Delilah the Dubious
> Sales Representative
> Round Products Division
> Imum Industries

"You can see what's going on, can't you? Imum doesn't have
enough capacity. It's giving Hercules Wagon extra wheels for that
Tower of Babel contract! It's favoritism! And now we're left in
the lurch for two to four weeks!" Cyrus exclaimed.

"The day after tomorrow," said Bibi, "we're going to have a
hundred wagons that can't be shipped to customers because they
don't have any wheels!"

"And when we met with Delilah to complain, her suggestion
was that we stockpile more inventory so that next time, this
doesn't happen!"

"I can barely stand to think about it," said Bibi. "Hundreds of
wagons up on blocks! Customers yelling at us because their wagons aren't ready! Managers glaring at us! Great wailing and
gnashing of teeth!"

"Is there anything you can do to help us?" asked Cyrus.

"Well . . . how many wheels do you need?"

"Four hundred by tomorrow afternoon."

"And another four hundred by the end of the week," added Bibi.

Ben swallowed hard. *That's a lot of wheels and not much time to
make them,* he thought. He was not even sure that Max's factory
had enough materials in stock. But he also knew that this was the
moment. He had to come through for them.

"Of course I can help you," he said. "You two go home and get
a good night's sleep. Let me worry about it."

In unison, Cyrus and Bibi let out sighs of relief. Ben shook their hands, walked calmly outside—and then sprinted for his chariot.

"Hee-yah!" he yelled to the horses. He raced to Max's wheel factory, cracking the whip as he went.

Minnie's Notes . . .

With builders and their customers, a deal worth millions might be closed with a simple hand-shake—because of mutual trust.

When he got there, Artemus, the factory supervisor, was just about to give his instructions to the evening-shift workers and go home for the night. As soon as he saw Ben the Builder striding toward him, he said to himself, "Uh-oh," and tried to disappear.

Ben, however, was too quick for him. He knew Art's escape route and headed him off. "Hold on, Art. I need to talk to you. I've got a rush order."

"How *rush* is it?"

"Very. I need four hundred wheels by tomorrow afternoon."

"What? No way! It's impossible!"

"Well, how many can you give me?"

"If they start on it first thing tomorrow morning," Artemus said, thinking, "maybe a hundred."

"Why tomorrow morning? Why can't you start tonight?"

"We're running the Jerusalem order tonight."

"Jerusalem can wait," Ben told him. "If they start tonight that'll be another hundred, plus the hundred from the day shift."

"You're going to ruin my schedule!"

But Ben was already wondering how many finished wheels they had in inventory. "I'm going to go check the warehouse. You'd better get them started on changing the setup."

"Changing the setup?!"

"The order is for solid wheels, not spoked."

"Agghh!"

Now, it was a sacred rule in manufacturing of that era (and often still is) that you never change a setup until a batch is completely finished. Wasting a setup, in Artemus's view, bordered on blasphemy.

"You can't do this to me!"

"I'm sorry, but this order is very, very important."

"So is efficiency!"

They began to argue, but then Max came out of his office and heard the commotion.

"What's going on?" Max demanded.

Ben explained.

Immediately, Max understood the importance. He looked at Artemus and said, "The future of the company could be at stake. Do what he says."

Artemus had to grit his teeth, but in the custom of the times, he bowed his head and turned to go give the instructions.

"And tell everyone they'll probably have to work later than usual," Max added. "We'll pay extra, but this job has to be finished on time."

Ben was already on his way to the warehouse. He found 160 solid wheels in stock, but they were tagged and ready to be shipped to Rome.

"I'm sorry, but you'll have to re-tag these for Atlas Wagons," Ben told the warehouse clerk.

"But these are supposed to go to catapult makers in Rome. The Romans are not going to be real happy about this."

"Ah, don't worry about the Romans. They're halfway across the Mediterranean Sea. What are they going to do to us?"

Meanwhile, on the factory floor, the work pace was picking up. Max and Minnie themselves were pitching in. Ben sent a messenger to tell his wife he might not be home for a while, then even he donned a leather apron and did what he could.

They worked all night. In the morning, Ben got a few hours of sleep in Max's office. When he woke up, the day-shift people were turning out the wheels.

By mid-afternoon, there they were: 240 lovely new wheels.

They had set a production record and completed an extra 40. With the 160 that had been confiscated from the Romans, the order was complete.

Just rounding up enough carts and wagons to deliver the order was a chore. Ben sat in the lead wagon. On the way to Atlas, he dozed.

As they brought the order into the factory, Cyrus and Bibi came out to inspect it—and to congratulate Ben the Builder.

"Thank you," said Cyrus. "We sure appreciate how you came through for us."

"You might have saved our careers," whispered Bibi.

"We will not forget this," said Cyrus.

And they didn't.

When Ben submitted the invoice, they didn't question the amount, even with the overtime.

Just a few weeks afterward, Atlas Wagon officially fired Imum Industries and named Max's Wheel Company as its regular supplier.

And it didn't even matter that Ben's price quote was a shekel or two higher per wheel than Imum's. After their "reliability concerns" regarding Imum, they knew that a few shekels one way or the other didn't matter. Ben the Builder was worth it.

So Max's began to deliver 1,200 wheels per month. This continued for six months, until the quantity was revised—upward, to 1,600 wheels. Six months after that, the number rose again, to 2,000 wheels a month. Together, the two companies, Atlas and Max's Wheel, began to grow in lockstep with each other.

Minnie's Notes . . .

Ozzie the Oracle's 6 Bedrock Questions— with Answers for a Builder Sales Market

1. Who are our customers?

- Experienced buyers (those who have bought wheels before and will buy them again and again).
- Often, in business-to-business selling, there is an "inside expert," someone on the customer's staff designated to handle this purchase because of prior experience with the product (e.g., a purchasing agent, but also a <u>function</u> manager, such as a data processing manager who specifies which computers to buy). There often are also <u>secondary</u> customers who have influence over the sale, ranging from the company president to the actual users of whatever is being purchased. These are people who can say <u>no</u> to the sale, but can't authoritatively say <u>yes</u>.

2. Who are our competitors?

- Our primary competition is from other companies selling essentially the same product or service, perhaps in slightly different configurations (i.e., Imum Industries). Eventually, though, we may face competition from companies selling new technology or radical, nonstandard improvements to current technology (some wizard who invents the Tire, for instance).

3. Why do customers want what we are selling?

- We sell a standard product (or a standard solution to a customer's problem), but by knowing the customer well, we can adapt features, options, delivery, support, etc. to each customer's individual needs.

4. What would make them prefer to buy from us?

- We have intimate knowledge of the customer's business and individual needs, and we have developed a level of trust between ourselves and the customer that cannot be easily duplicated or disrupted.

(continued)

5. Why might they prefer to buy from our competitors?
- If we screw up, the bond of trust will be broken and they will consider alternatives. Likewise, if they learn of a competitor offering dramatically lower prices for essentially the same goods and services, they might begin to question their loyalty.

6. What added values does our salesperson have to offer to make a sale?
- The salesperson must be able to build trusting relationships with key people on the customer's side. He or she has to be able to manage complexity, keep close watch on the details; must be a customer advocate inside the seller's organization; and must have the clout to disrupt internal routines when necessary to keep the customer happy. Above all, the salesperson adds value to a conventional product through personal attentions lavished upon the customer.

21

The key to Ben the Builder's success as a salesman was based on the success of his customers. He was always looking for ways to help his customers do better.

Ben treated his customers almost like business partners. That is, Ben was always looking for ways to help his customers succeed. Because if he could do that, he could ensure his own success.

One day, Ben had a meeting with Cyrus and Bibi in which Cyrus remarked to Bibi, "You know, I was talking to Wendell, and he doesn't know what he's going to do with all the Plums."

"Plums?" asked Ben.

"Yeah, remember all those purple wheels we ordered? We call 'em Plums. Well, they're not selling. Nobody wants a wagon with big purple

> ## Minnie's Notes . . .
>
> Builders are the backbone of most business-to-business selling.

wheels on it. Wendell says he's got thousands of Plums filling the warehouse and he doesn't know what to do. It's really a problem."

Ben the Builder, of course, knew that this was indeed a problem. Thousands of unsellable plum-colored wheels were the equivalent of hundreds of thousands of shekels in cost.

Now, certainly neither Cyrus nor Bibi blamed Ben for the problem. After all, Atlas had dictated to him the color choices— and Ben had dutifully worked with the paint shop in Max's wheel factory to get an exact match to the swatches Cyrus had given him. Indeed, Ben had kept the paint shop people laboring very late one night just to get that perfect plum hue. Trouble was, wagon buyers hated the color and had walked away in droves.

"You know, I can't promise anything," Ben said to Cyrus and Bibi, "but let me see what I can do."

He went back to the paint shop at Max's factory and asked how much it would cost to repaint all the Plums in some other color. The shop boss gave him the figure of five shekels a wheel.

Next, Ben went to another customer he'd been courting for some time, a specialty wagon maker who had given him a few small orders, but nothing major as yet.

Minnie's Notes . . .

Builders seldom offer the customer a rock-bottom price. But by looking out for their customers' best interests, builders can more than justify the slightly higher prices they quote.

"Listen," said Ben, "I've got a special deal for you." And he explained that a certain other customer of his had some extra wheels that couldn't be used at present. "We can refurbish these wheels so they're as good as new. If you agree to take the whole lot of them, and you're flexible about delivery, I'll give you the normal discount from list price, plus a one-time-only extra discount of five shekels a wheel."

Done. The specialty wagon maker took the deal in a heartbeat.

So Ben the Builder went back to Cyrus and Bibi and said, "Tell you what: I'll take the Plums back and give you full credit for them, minus a five-shekel-per-wheel restocking fee."

"You will?" exclaimed Cyrus.

"What a relief," said Bibi.

In the end, everyone was happy.

Atlas Wagons got rid of its Plums. It was happy to pay the five shekels per wheel, because that was a heck of a lot better than having to write off hundreds of thousands of shekels.

The five shekels paid to keep the paint shop busy during slow times between regular production work.

And the specialty wagon maker got a huge supply of an essential component at a terrific price, helping to make it all the more profitable over the long haul.

Above all, the word got around at Atlas Wagon that Ben was the kind of guy who would go the extra mile for you.

Yet Ben the Builder didn't stop there.

Sometime after the Plum incident, Ben the Builder got to wondering: Was there some way that they could avoid that kind of problem in the future? Suppose next time Atlas ordered Lemon Yellow Wheels and they proved to be as popular as the Plums?

So Ben had an idea. He went to Minnie and said, "You know, I've been thinking about how we might prevent all that running around we did with the Plum-Painted Wheels."

"How's that?" asked Minnie.

"We'll offer them—and ourselves—a leg up."

"A leg up?"

"I suggest we hire a sage and we have that sage do research on what wagon buyers value most in a wheel."

"But why would *we* want to do that?"

"Two reasons," said Ben. "First, it will give us an edge on our competition. With sage research, we will know in advance which features and options we should be adding to our wheels, so we'll

Minnie's Notes . . .

A builder's biggest challenge is to keep finding ways to add value to the sale, in the face of increasing parity between competing products. And it's critical that the seller document cost savings (or revenue gains) for the buyer. Often, a seller that's performing well isn't noticed by the buyer's organization.

be able to bring to the market each year a wheel that's better than last year's wheel.

"Second, we can turn that research into a selling tool. By sharing what we learn with Atlas and perhaps a few other of our best customers, we can show them what kinds of wheels they ought to be buying—and if they do buy accordingly, that should simplify everything for them."

Minnie thought a moment and asked, "Well, it sounds good, but what about the cost?"

"We're talking about our biggest and best customers here. The services of one lousy sage are nothing compared with those. We can easily absorb the cost—and if we can use this research to convince them to buy wheels with extra features, our sales and our profits can only increase."

"All right," said Minnie, "let's do it."

So Ben the Builder engaged the services of the best market-research sage he could find. Sometime later, based on the sage's findings, Atlas's luxury wagons began sporting big, red-rimmed wheels with gold spokes.

Well, the reaction was overwhelming. Wagon buyers everywhere went wild over the new two-tone wheels.

Within a month, Atlas had doubled the original order it had placed with Ben—and tripled it two months after that. That year, *both* Atlas Wagon and Max's Wheel Company had record sales and profits.

◆   ◆   ◆

There were some who thought that Ben got business just because he was a good-time guy. These people, however, were very mistaken.

Yes, Ben was a warm human being. His big smile came easy to him, his handshake was always firm, and when appropriate he would even slap the back of a toga or two.

Ben would almost always pick up the tab for lunch down at the Camel Club. He was forever taking people to Gladiator games, or to the crocodile races, or to the galley regattas. And his recall of ancient jokes was legend among all who knew him.

Yet at the core of Ben the Builder was a strong work ethic. In truth, Ben got business because, above all, he made it possible for other people and their companies to be more productive, have fewer problems, and earn more shekels.

Ben the Builder never stopped looking for ways—large and small—that would strengthen the bond between the customer and himself. Indeed, this was why he was named Ben the Builder:

Ben built relationships . . .

Which built his accounts . . .

Which built market share . . .

Which built wealth.

Within the year, Atlas Wagon had adopted Max's Spoked Wheel as an available option on its top-of-the-line Colossus model. By the end of two years, Max's Spoked Wheel had become an option on the entire line of wagons, from the entry-level Spartan to the mid-priced Blue Nile Special.

Furthermore, Spoked Wheels had become the standard wheel offered on both the luxury Colossus and the high-performance Ramses Sport Wagon.

Indeed, Atlas Wagon soon became the largest single customer ever of Max's Wheel Company—bigger even than Wheels sold during the Great Pyramid project. While Max's company had sold hundreds and hundreds of Wheels to help build the Great

Pyramid, Atlas Wagon was buying thousands and thousands. Such was the impact of Ben the Builder.

Ozzie's Insights . . .

Top Characteristics of a
World Class Builder Sales Force

- World Class builder salespeople have detailed personal knowledge not only of their individual customers, but also of the complexities of those customers' businesses.
- A "do whatever it takes" attitude. Fast response.
- A focus on accounts, not projects.
- A management willing to invest time and resources in developing relationships with customers. They invest the most, of course, in the customers likely to spend the most.
- An identification with the customer; a sense of being the customers' advocates inside the seller's organization.
- A willingness to disrupt internal policies and efficiencies for the benefit of the customer.
- World Class builders keep pace with technical change. Even though they are not technically expert themselves, they know where and how to get technical expertise—fast—when their customers require it.
- The World Class builder sales forces tend to organize themselves to fit the customers they can best serve. Often this is by size of their customers' organizations—small, medium, and large—and they gear their internal systems and resources accordingly.
- An organizational ability to let go of customers and markets when it becomes impossible to service them profitably and competitively.
- Common liabilities: too much identification with the customer; advocacy of the customer at the expense of the seller's financial health; too conservative in the face of technological change.

Part Four

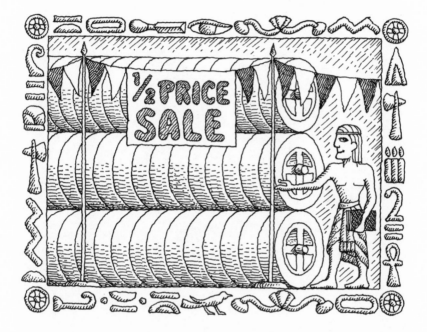

BILLIONS
AND BILLIONS
OF WHEELS!

22

One day, when the future could not have looked brighter, Max took a moment to sit back, put his sandals on the corner of his desk, and read the paper.

Scanning the sports section, a story caught his eye (the Tigris Tigers had beaten the Jericho Blue Jays, 24–14), and when he turned the page to read the end of it, he could not help but notice a big, full-page ad with screaming headlines: WHEELS! ONLY 49.99!

As Max read that ad, his eyes got big and his stomach turned sour.

Right away, he went to find Minnie.

"Have you seen this?" he asked.

Minnie scanned the ad and admitted, "My, but that is a great price. And they look just like our wheels."

"Minnie, they're cloning our wheels! They're knocking them off with low-priced labor in China and bringing them in by caravan!"

"Let's go find Ben and see what he knows."

So they found Ben the Builder, who was telling the other salespeople about the sporty new chariot he'd just bought for his son, Buddy.

"Excuse me, but we need to have a word with you," said Minnie.

"What's the problem?"

They stepped aside, and Max showed Ben the ad—to which Ben the Builder just laughed.

WHEELS!!!
ONLY 49.99!

SIZES TO FIT ALL STANDARD AXLES!
LOTS OF GREAT COLORS:
RED, BLUE, PURPLE, GOLD, AND
POPULAR TWO-TONE COMBINATIONS!
HOT OFF THE CARAVAN FROM CHINA!
30-DAY MONEY-BACK GUARANTEE!
WE PROUDLY ACCEPT
COLOSSUS CHARGE CARD & ROMAN EXPRESS

EXCELSIOR WHEEL WAREHOUSE
FOR ALL YOUR OXCART,
WAGON, & CHARIOT NEEDS

"What's to worry about?" Ben asked. "At those prices, they'll never stay in business!"

"Are you sure?" asked Max.

"Absolutely! Besides, those wheels are probably damaged or faulty somehow. There is no way that they could offer quality wheels like ours at that kind of price. Somebody on the other side of the Himalayas got stuck with a bad batch or too much inventory and decided to unload. That's all."

"Whew, that's a relief," said Minnie.

"And anyway," Ben continued, "my relationship with Atlas Wagon is rock solid. They'll never find anyone to take care of them like I do."

Within a few short years, it was painfully obvious to Max, Minnie, Ben the Builder, and everyone else that wheels imported from across the Himalayas were not inferior to those produced by Max's company or any other of the Big Wheelers.

Some even claimed that wheels made in China were *superior* in quality—though actually the quality in measurable terms was about the same.

What was definitely not the same was the price. The first caravan of imported cloned wheels sold for fifty shekels, twenty percent less than the best discount price for Max's comparable wheels. And, contrary to the prediction of Ben the Builder, the seller did not lose money.

In six months, the price had dropped further—to thirty-nine shekels a wheel. And six months after that, the "Dead Sea" price for wheels was twenty-nine shekels.

"Twenty-nine shekels!" shouted Max. "How can they do that? Twenty-nine shekels is under half what we were charging our best customers just a year ago!"

And though everyone denied it would ever happen, sure enough, it did. At first it was just the marginal accounts that strayed. These were smaller customers who, under Ben's way of selling, got less attention than, say, the customers of Atlas Wagon stature. These customers began to say to themselves, "Hey, a wheel is a wheel. Why pay more?"

As they began to drift from Max's company customer list, Ben all but said good riddance.

"Look," Ben did in fact say, "we weren't making that much money on them anyway. We've still got the Golden Customers. We've still got the high end of the wheel market, the really desirable segment, like Atlas. We've never lost a customer we really wanted to keep, and we never will."

The next time he called upon Atlas Wagon, Ben was a few minutes early, so he was shown to Cyrus's office to wait until Cyrus and Bibi were free. And there on Cyrus's desk, he saw a newspaper opened to yet another full-page ad for Excelsior Wheel Warehouse, this one shrieking:

WHEELS
ONLY 24 SHEKELS!

Ben the Builder knew this was not a good sign.

When his customers arrived, their faces were as grim as Pluto's shadow.

"How's it going?" Ben asked pleasantly.

"Good for us," said Cyrus.

"Not so good for you," said Bibi.

"Why is that?"

"Ben, we need to talk."

"And, Ben, understand that what we have to say is no reflection on you."

"What's going on? We've been doing business together for a long time now. If there's a problem, I'm sure we can work it out."

"I hope so," said Cyrus.

"We've found out the hard way," said Bibi, "that the Hercules Wagon Company is buying its wheels direct from Excelsior. Their whole new line is priced a good ten to fifteen percent below our comparable models, and it's mainly because they've got a better price on their wheels."

"Yes, a much better price."

"So, we have no choice, Ben. We have to do the same thing or we're going to lose market share."

"Wait, wait! Hold on here!" said Ben, summoning a smile. "If it's just a question of a few shekels—"

"It's not just a few, Ben. Excelsior quoted us a price of twenty-two shekels—an even ten below your price."

"But . . . but can't you see? They're just doing it to get your business!" Yet as Ben the Builder scanned their faces, it seemed that Excelsior's ploy may well have succeeded.

"I had to match the price!" Ben said to Max and Minnie. "They are our best Golden Customer!"

"But, Ben," said Max, "if we sell them wheels at twenty-four shekels, we're gonna lose money on every wheel we sell!"

"I know, but we'll make it up on volume!" said Ben, uttering a remark that would echo forward through the centuries.

At this point, Ben, who had practically been on his knees in front of Max and Minnie, pleading his case, straightened up and said, "If we don't keep our customers, then we lose the company anyway."

Max turned away. He felt his world spinning. After all he had done, a bunch of commodity clones was about to take it away.

He turned to Minnie. "What can we do?"

The Oracle awakened to a certain aroma, the likes of which he had not enjoyed in quite some time. He followed his nose to the front of the cave, where he found the usual small fire—and Max and Minnie. On a stone slab over the hot coals baked something round, red, and cheesy.

"Here you have it," said Max with a flourish, "a large pizza with the works."

The Oracle rubbed his hand together. "Oooo! Thank you!"

The old man sat down, tossed his long white beard over his shoulder lest he stain it with spilled tomato sauce and melted cheese, and helped himself.

"I don't know why," he said, "but they just won't deliver to me up here."

After putting away half the pie, the Oracle said, "So it's been a while. How are things in the wheel business?"

"Terrible," said Minnie.

"Terrible for us at least," said Max. "Not so long ago, our company was the market leader. Next year, we'll be lucky just to be in the market."

"What's happened?" asked the Oracle.

"Cheap clones," said Minnie. She told the old man everything that had taken place since their last visit, and concluded, "We just can't compete anymore. Yesterday we almost lost our best Golden Customer over price, and the way things are headed, we might not have *any* customers very soon."

"But you still do have customers?" asked the Oracle.

"Oh, yes."

"Who are the most profitable ones?"

"Mostly," said Minnie, "they're the ones who want something

special. Like maybe they want wheels that are a special size. Or they want wheels for a special application—you know, that will hold up going across a desert or someplace. Or maybe they want wheels with a particular paint job that no one else has."

The Oracle nodded. "That's good. That means your business will probably be able to survive by serving needs that others have ignored.

"But, first of all, no matter what else, you need to lower your costs. That's absolutely a must in order to compete at this stage of the market. You have to have a lean organization and highly efficient manufacturing. That's top priority. Now, assuming you can do that, you have some choices."

"Well, that is a relief," said Max. "I wasn't sure we had *any* options."

"Oh, yes, you do have a few. Once again, though, you need to make a strategic decision. Because, basically, you have two choices: You can seek a market niche in special types of wheels. Or you can seek to dominate the wheel mass market."

Without hesitation, Max answered, "I want the second. I want my company to dominate the mass market."

"Not so fast," said the Oracle. "Let me tell you, there is nothing wrong with being a niche player. It may represent your best prospects. If you chose to be a specialty wheel maker, you could simply refocus the company and trim it to a smaller size. You would have to accept lower volume and sales revenue, but you could still be very profitable."

"No," said Max. "I want us to be the market leader we used to be."

"Then you're going to have to make sacrifices, the first one being Ben the Builder."

"But why?" asked Minnie. "Ben is the best!"

"He was the best in yesterday's market. Not anymore. Today, Ben and the other builders are too expensive for what most customers need, and their selling style is inefficient in this market—a market of commodity wheels."

Max was taken aback, even offended. "You're saying the wheel, my Wheel, is . . . a commodity?"

"Face it. It's true; wheels are a commodity. They have the same standard features. Nobody needs any special expertise to use them. All the Big Wheelers offer about the same manufacturing quality. Even you admit that the wheels coming in from China are clones—essentially the same as what you produce. They only differentiating factor is price."

Agitated, Max paced about the cave. "Commodity! But I don't want us to be in a commodity market!"

"You know," said the Oracle, "lots of businesspeople say that. They say, 'We don't want to be in a commodity market.' Like there is some kind of stigma attached. And yet, this kind of a market is where really big money can be made. Sell a billion commodity wheels and, even if you make only a single shekel on each one, you've made a billion shekels."

The thought of a billion shekels in profit made the idea of a commodity market more palatable to Max.

"Okay," he said. "What do we have to do to dominate the market?"

"You're probably not going to like this, but you're going to have to focus not on great salespeople, but on a great sales system."

"What do you mean by that?"

"You'll have to move Ben and the other builders aside, cut their number, keeping only the very best, and put them in charge of specialty wheels, where the margins can support the kind of individual attention they lavish on their customers.

"In their place, you'll have to build an entire new sales organization with people who are skilled, but who are much lower cost than the builders and are easily replaceable. Rather than sales professionals, think of them as a sales crew—as people who work together as a team.

"You'll want to have procedures in place to recruit and train these people quickly so you can add more when the business expands—but also because, frankly, you won't be able to pay any of them great money and it's inevitable that you're going to have turnover.

"You do want them to be well trained because to dominate in this market, you're going to have to offer unbeatable customer service. But you're also going to have to come up with noncash incentives to motivate the sales crew, incentives that are effective, but don't cost a lot."

"Wow, that is a big change," said Minnie. Then, turning to Max, she added, "But you're the CEO. It's up to you."

"My mind is made up," said Max. "I want to beat the clone-makers. I want us to be at the top, the way we were not so very long ago."

"All right," said the Oracle, "but to beat them you'll have to join them."

On their way back down the mountain, Max said to Minnie, "If we need to move Ben aside, who should replace him?"

"Well," said Minnie, after thinking for a minute, "the Oracle told us that we need to think of our salespeople in the new market as being 'crew.' So it seems to me that if we have a crew, we need to have a captain."

"You mean a 'Captain of Sales'?"

"Um, yes . . ." Minnie looked at Max. "Say, why is that name familiar?"

After an extensive search, Max and Minnie found Caleb, the Captain of Sales, and met with him harborside in the great trading port of Rhodes, where he was now sales manager of a discount superstore chain.

After listening to their offer (which was for a great deal of money), the Captain stoked his chin. "Okay, your offer is generous. But why do you think that things would be any better now than they were the first time?"

"When we first got together so many years ago," said Minnie, "we didn't know it and you didn't know it, but the approach you took was exactly wrong for the age of the product we were selling and for the type of customer we needed to sell to. Now, we believe that your approach is exactly right."

The Captain nodded again. "It's going to be a big challenge. The cloners have a real price advantage."

"We're talking to wizards right now who can put some magic into our manufacturing to raise productivity and bring down costs. Before long, we should be able to narrow the gap."

"I'll have to make a lot of changes, reinvent the sales culture. I'm going to need your support and a lot of control."

"You'll have it," said Minnie.

They came to an arrangement, and within a fairly short time, Caleb, the Captain of Sales, was on the job, assembling his crew.

23

Ben the Builder was outraged.

"You should see his new ad campaign!" he complained to his wife. "It's awful!"

"Whose new ad campaign?"

"The new guy, my replacement, the so-called Captain of Sales! Ha! He's not worthy to be captain of a rowboat!"

"You say it's *his* campaign?"

"Well, no, it's the company's. But he's the one who approved it. He and Minnie."

"What's so bad about it?"

"There's nothing to it, no substance! Every ad is just a brand name and some feel-good words and pictures!"

Indeed, the newly hired ad agency had come up with a completely new product trademark: MaxWheels.

And the agency was plastering it everywhere. From the Blue Nile to the Black Sea, billboards in every kingdom and empire were emblazoned with the new design and the slogan: "MaxWheels! Roll On!"

Then there was what became famous as "the Chariot Ad." It was a painting of four snorting, charging white horses pulling a golden chariot, racing ahead of others in the background, with the bold, stern-jawed charioteer holding the reins in one hand while in the other he held aloft a streaming banner proclaiming "MaxWheels! Roll On!" The ad appeared everywhere—and, hey, it even took first place in the Cleo Awards.

Meanwhile, Phil the Phlack had been given new duties. Used to be, back in Toby the Wizard's heyday, Phil had worked to get exposure through means like publishing by-lined technical articles, creating seminars, and booking speaking engagements. Later, when Ben took over, Phil had cajoled editors of trade magazines like *Wagon Week* to do case histories on things that Max's company did just a little bit better than others, things like inventory-control services and paint selection. And there had been the highbrow, do-good events like Max's Wheel Company's Celebrity Wagon Roll for Lepers.

Minnie's Notes . . .

WHen markets mature, product improvements are incremental rather than revolutionary—a lot of small steps forward rather than big technological leaps. Once a technology matures and products based on it achieve parity with one another, it becomes increasingly difficult to make radical advances, because customers expect standards to be observed, and because commodity prices do not allow margins to justify big development expenses.

"And now," said Ben, "what's Phil the Phlack doing *now*? He's trying to get 'MaxWheels' painted on the side of the Great Pyramid!"

"No! They're not going to do that, are they?" asked his wife.

"Not likely. The Pharaoh's business agents want too many

shekels. But the Tower of Babel is interested. They're trying to build that monstrosity all the way to Heaven, and they're almost bankrupt."

In truth, Phil was also engaged in a number of other activities to build visibility for the brand—like getting MaxWheels named as the Official Wheel Supplier for the World Championship Chariot Races.

"You know, in my day," said Ben, "we'd run ads that weren't just fluff! Remember the one about how our wheels didn't squeak 'cause they used grease?"

"But, Ben," said his wife, "today *every* wheel maker's wheels use grease."

"That's not the point!"

Unfortunately, whether Ben wanted to admit it or not, that was very much the point. There was precious little about wheels these days to distinguish one maker's brand from another.

In order to reduce costs, options had been reduced (because every option offered on the product usually meant an increase in production and inventory expenses). In Ben's day, you could get your wheel spokes in all kinds of different shapes—round, square, octagonal, or carved in the shape of your favorite demigod. You could get the spokes gold-plated, or in molded bronze, or in polished copper, or in plain old wood. Now, wheel spokes were almost always wood, and they were either round or square. Everything else cost too much.

Same with colors. Ben used to keep with him in his chariot a lavishly produced book of color samples. Max's Wheel Company once offered wheels in 1,000 different colors. Now, the customer could choose from any of a dozen colors, so long as they were in stock. And Max had market sages on retainer investigating how they could reduce those dozen shades down to the eight most popular.

So, in fairness, the creative scribes at the new ad agency—Nefertiti & Jones—didn't have much to work with. Were they supposed to write in the ad copy "Buy our wheels because they're the same as all the others?"

Hence, the new trademark. Hence, the spending to build awareness of the MaxWheels brand.

But what outraged Ben the Builder the very most was the kind of salespeople the captain was hiring.

"What's wrong with them?" asked his wife.

"They're not really salespeople!" stormed Ben. "They're . . . they're just a bunch of kids!"

In a sense, he was right. The people being hired by the Captain for sales positions were not in the same league as Ben the Builder or any of the salespeople of his caliber.

They didn't know about things like qualifying a customer. Most of them thought that "answering objections" was something a trial lawyer did. And as Ben asserted, many of them "couldn't close a sale if their lives depended on it."

At least, not when they started working for the company.

The kind of people hired by the Captain tended to be young. They were normal to good-looking in appearance. They were of average to slightly above-average intelligence. They were somewhat educated—though there were no scholars among them.

More important, they had personalities and dispositions that were friendly and pleasant. They had good attitudes. They were upbeat. And, above all, they had excellent people skills. They weren't subject to "social fatigue."

The Captain searched for those who could socialize quickly and easily. He wanted people who could talk comfortably even with total strangers. He also wanted people who could listen, who could empathize with the needs and situations of those whom they had never met before and might personally never meet again.

You see, the Captain of Sales did not care if the individual salesperson bonded with the individual customer. In fact, the Captain often quietly discouraged such things. What mattered was each customer's relationship with the MaxWheels brand.

Indeed, inside the company, the Captain didn't even call them salespeople. He called them his "sales crew"—and thought of them as being like the crew of a ship.

Adam, Sarah, Josephine, and Tom were four members of the Captain's crew. They worked at the new MaxWheels MegaMart that had just opened in the ancient yet bustling city of Tyre.

Ben the Builder would have called them "kids," though they were not. They were mostly in their twenties and early thirties, and they typically had little to no sales experience.

Previous work in sales didn't matter to the Captain—so long as they had the other qualities that made them worth hiring. In fact, the Captain almost preferred that this be their first sales job, because that way he didn't have to break any bad habits. He could train them according to his own discipline.

The Captain's training program was brief but concentrated. All of the crew went through it—and not just once, but periodically, as it came time to learn new things.

They learned the simple stuff, like how to greet the customer. They practiced engaging the customer in easy conversation, at first about everyday things like the weather and sports, but quickly advancing to learning their tastes and needs with respect to wheels.

Even more important than talking, they learned how to listen. Then they would use what they heard to continue the conversation, all the while sorting out what this customer really wanted.

By the middle of the conversation, the Captain's crew member would know which issues and features were really important to getting this customer's business and which were less important or even irrelevant. Did this person want wheels with style? Or were function and price the main concerns?

Now, you should understand that in those days (as is often the case today), many wheel vendors did not invest in their employees. That is, after the employees were hired, they usually were just trained on the job by someone who was often only slightly more experienced than the new kid.

On top of everything else, the Captain's crew learned real closing skills. These were fairly easily learned—and simple, yet effective.

For instance, he taught them the time-honored "Yes" close. The way it worked simply was to ask the customer questions to which the easy answer for each was yes. After half a dozen or so of these, a pattern had been established and the customer was all the more likely to say yes to the sale.

When Adam greeted a customer, he would open with a question about the weather, like: "Nice day out there, isn't it?"

"Sure is," the customer would say.

"Looking for some new wheels?"

"Yes, I am."

"They're going to go on that fast-looking chariot you just arrived in?"

"Yep!"

"Are you looking for wheels that offer performance at an affordable price?"

"You bet."

"Here they are," Adam would say, "the Ben Hur Specials. Would you like the free mounting and balancing?"

"Absolutely!"

And that was that—the sale was made.

Even easier than the "Yes" close was the "Friendly Assumption" close. Josephine used this a lot. Essentially, while waiting on a customer, she would carry on a friendly conversation and assume that the customer would buy the wheels she selected. It was a close so subtle that it seldom appeared to be a close at all.

One afternoon, there was a customer browsing through the

racks of wheels. He asked Josephine, "Excuse me, do these wheels come in the color green?"

"Would you like them in green?"

"Umm, yes, I think I would."

"Let's take a look down here. Say, that's a nice toga you're wearing."

"Thank you."

"With the holidays coming up, I was thinking about getting my brother a new toga, but he's so hard to buy for. Oh, here we are, green wheels. Very nice shade, too. Do you buy your togas in town?"

"Umm, yeah, I get them down at a shop on the corner of Pyramis and Thisbe Streets."

"Do they have a nice selection?"

"I've always been happy with it," said the customer.

All the while, Josephine was rolling the green wheels up the aisle to the front of the store. Still making idle conversation, she began writing up the order. And the sale was painlessly made.

Now, if the customer objected, saying something like "Wait a minute. Hold it. I'm not really sure I want green," then Josephine would simply reply, "Oh, I'm sorry! No problem. Say, what's your favorite color?"

"Blue."

"Would you like these in blue?"

"Umm, sure."

And on she would go.

But for all the dozens upon dozens of closing techniques that had been devised over the centuries, the Captain knew that the best way to get continuing sales was to effectively resolve every customer's two main, fundamental reasons for not buying.

Whenever people in this type of market think about buying

something, they silently, perhaps unknowingly, ask themselves a couple of questions.

First: Is this really the best price?

And, second: Is buying here going to be a hassle?

Naturally, to get the sale, the answer to the first question has to be *yes* and the answer to the second has to be *no*—and the more definitely the salesperson can make assurances to that effect, the more likely potential buyers will be to part with their shekels.

So, to deal with the question of price, the Captain would have each MegaMart's crew do things to ease customers' anxiety over whether they were really getting a good deal.

For instance, he might have the crew post the ads of competitors—along with evidence showing that MaxWheels were the best deal around. This way, aside from keeping everyone on their toes with respect to keeping prices low, they could prove to the customer that there was no need to shop further.

Of course, competition being what it was, the MaxWheels MegaMarts didn't always have the very best price—not if they wanted to stay profitable. So the Captain authorized the On-the-Spot Discount. If customers came into the store, but indicated that they were not convinced that MaxWheels were a terrific value, any member of the sales crew could authorize a one-shekel-per-wheel discount—if the crew member thought it would clinch the sale.

If you're in a market in which competition is based largely on price, one very important thing to keep in mind is which, if any, services are bundled with the sale. As the Captain knew, services cost shekels, and often the best policy is to offer a low product price and charge separately for any services associated with the sale—like, in the case of wheels, the services of putting them on the customers' wagons, ox carts, and chariots.

But there were times when the crew could use services to demonstrate better value. When confronted with a wheel store offering a ridiculously low price per wheel, the crew could often point out, "Yeah, they only want nineteen shekels a wheel, but they'll charge you another ten to mount them on your wagon. Here you pay twenty shekels a wheel—but only five to put them on."

Still, even though price was always an issue to every wheel buyer, it was never the only factor. Just as important was making the sale *easy*.

All customers wanted a wheel-buying experience that was problem-free. They wanted wheels with good manufacturing quality. They wanted wheels that would be reliable. Beyond the product itself, however, they wanted the sales transaction to be easy.

"You keep saying we have to keep making it easier for the customer," Minnie said to the Captain one day when they were having a meeting. "How much easier can we make it?"

"I really don't know," said the Captain, "but we have to keep trying."

"But why? Shouldn't we be focusing more on lowering the price?"

"Look, it comes down to this: The main trick in this market is do everything possible to remove the barriers to the sale."

"Barriers? What kinds of barriers?"

"Well, in one sense, price is a barrier. It's a point of resistance that potentially keeps the customer from buying. A lower price means lower resistance. A higher price means more resistance. It causes people to think twice; it slows things down. But price is only one barrier.

"These days, everybody with a wagon, a cart, or a chariot needs to buy new wheels from time to time. But whose wheels will they buy? Our wheels, realistically speaking, are about the same as Imum's or anyone else's. And they're all roughly the same price. What, then, determines the customer's choice? Convenience. The seller who makes the purchase easiest for the individual customer gets the sale.

"Now, in order to understand convenience, you have to look

at the opposite: inconvenience. So we have to ask, what can cause the customer inconvenience?

"One cause of inconvenience is distance. If the store is too far away from the customer, the sale is not convenient. So we build as many stores as close to as many different customers as we can efficiently run.

"What else can make a sale inconvenient? Time—or the lack thereof. Even worse, we make things inconvenient if we *waste* the customer's time. Like if somebody comes into the store and can't get helped right away. Or if it takes hours of waiting until we can get the new wheels put onto the customer's wagon."

"Or," said Minnie, "if they come in and we don't have the exact wheel that they need."

"Right. If we're out of stock, or don't carry a broad enough inventory, then we've wasted the customer's time. Another huge

If the barrier is . . .	Resolve it with . . .
High price	Easy credit
	Installment payments
	Discounts
Distance	Convenient locations
	Free delivery
	Catalogues
Lack of time	Faster service
	Efficient store layout
	Streamlined checkout
	Broad inventory
	One-stop shopping
Bad experience	Sympathetic employees
	No-hassle exchanges

source of inconvenience is a problem after the sale—say, a wheel breaks after only a week of use. If we don't deal with the problem and make it right, then we're creating bad memories. A customer's bad memories and bad feelings are among the worst and hardest barriers to remove—not only to the one sale, obviously, but to future and continuing sales.

"Listen, you don't have to be Aristotle to figure out the barriers to sales. The difficult part is coming up with low-cost—or no-cost—ways to reduce or eliminate them. The seller who is best able to do that is the one who will ultimately dominate this market."

"Always remember that human nature tends to favor the easiest course of action," the Captain was fond of saying. "True, there will always be a rare few who will climb the mountain. But most will follow the road *around* the mountain. Therefore, don't build your business on the top of the mountain. Build it next to the road."

24

Coming up with ways to make things easier for the customer can be hard work.

Yet it was the kind of work the Captain insisted had to be done—and he never seemed to tire of doing it.

He was forever looking for ways to make the process of sales and service simpler, less aggravating, and more convenient. And he was always enlisting the help of his crew to create those ways.

One day, the Captain of Sales was visiting the MegaMart in Tyre, and he challenged each of the crew to come up with one good, new way to make something easier for the MaxWheels customer.

"And when I come back next month, I'm going to sit down and talk with each of you about your idea—or ideas, if you have more than one."

Now, *easier*, in the Captain's terms, had a broad meaning. It meant, of course, making things more convenient for the customer. But it also could mean adding some new procedure for dealing better with a common problem. Or, best of all, something to prevent a problem from happening. Or *easier* might mean a special new service—provided it didn't run up costs. A lot of times *easier* meant some new behavior on the part of the crew that would help the customer in some way.

It was at this point that Josephine said to him, "Wow, you must really love our customers."

The Captain looked at her kind of funny. He concluded that maybe she was looking for points with him by saying this. Or maybe she was just inspired by the moment. Either way, the Captain thought her comment was kind of mushy and off the mark.

"Love our customers? I don't think so."

"But you keep working—and you want us to keep working—to make things better for them."

"Yeah," said Adam. "You keep working for lower prices, more convenience. Why else would you be doing it?"

"Let me put it this way," said the Captain. "I love my wife. I love my kids. But customers? I can honestly say that I don't know the names of any of them.

"Yet I can also honestly say that each individual customer is important to me. Customers are to us what the rivers and the rains are to the farmer. If the Nile doesn't flood its banks each spring, the crops don't grow. If customers don't show up in our store, we don't grow. And if we don't grow . . ."

The Captain left them with that thought and headed up the coast to the grand opening of the MaxWheels MegaMart in Byblos. While he was gone, Adam, who was the crew leader, made sure that during the slow times of the day—usually in the middle of the afternoon—the crew members took time to kick around ideas on how to make things easier for the customer.

When the Captain returned the following month, each of the crew members had at least one idea to give, and several had half a dozen or more. Granted, a number of the ideas weren't very good,

Minnie's Notes . . .

Ozzie the Oracle's 6 Bedrock Questions—with Answers for a Captain-and-Crew Sales Market

1. Who are our customers?
- Experienced buyers with no requirements for major customization of the purchase. In business-to-business selling, they are typically some type of administrator, such as a purchasing agent or a clerk of some sort. In a retail market, the customers are typically called "consumers."

2. Who are our competitors?
- Others selling, for all practical purposes, the exact same thing

3. Why do customers want what we are selling?
- It's the standard, established solution

4. What would make them prefer to buy from us?
- Low price
- We're convenient
- Habit

5. Why might they prefer to buy from our competitors?
- A bad experience with us, sometimes even a minor one. Or an even <u>lower</u> price. Or better service, greater convenience.

6. What added values do our salespeople have to offer to make a sale?
- Our salespeople have to differentiate us from the competition—and add value to the commodity being sold—by offering superior service, yet also they must be efficient in so doing. Have to create a positive experience for each customer, and do so on a consistent basis.

and a few were just plain stupid. But the Captain listened to them all.

First he talked to Tom.

"My idea is that we should build a bigger store."

"Why is that?"

"Well, it gets kind of crowded in here sometimes, and a bigger store would give customers more elbow room."

"But we just built this store," said the Captain. "We can't afford another one."

"Oh."

"Why don't you think about how we might adjust some of the shelving. If you can come up with a more efficient layout, maybe we can ease the congestion without spending any more money."

"Hmmm," said Tom. "Okay."

Next, the Captain talked to Sarah. "What's your idea?"

"I think we should paint the whole store purple."

The Captain struggled not to roll his eyes. "Purple?"

"Yes, purple," she said.

"And, ah, exactly how is that going to make it easier for the customer to do business with us?"

"Well, you see, there are no other stores in all of Tyre that are painted purple. So this store would stand out. That would make it easier for customers to find us. We might even become a landmark. And, don't forget, the city of Tyre is famous throughout the world for its purple dyes. Kings and queens use those dyes to color their robes, and Tyrian purple is the color of royalty. If we painted the store that color, we'd be showing our civic pride, we'd be saying in a colorful way that we are the most noble choice in wheels, and therefore we'd make it easier for the customer to feel great about buying wheels from us."

With this explanation, the Captain nodded thoughtfully. What had at first seemed like a dumb idea maybe wasn't so dumb after all.

"All right. Sometime during off-peak hours, figure out how much it would cost to do that," he told Sarah.

Then came Josephine, who said, "I've seen a lot of customers walk out of the store when we tell them it'll take an hour or more to get their new wheels put onto their wagons and chariots. Waiting isn't easy for customers. So why don't we do whatever we can to shorten or eliminate the wait for them?"

The Captain, now, really liked what he was hearing. "Great. Do you have any specific suggestions?"

"Yes, I do. Why don't we guarantee that the wait will be less than an hour? If it's more than an hour, then we'll promise that we'll waive the service charges for mounting and balancing the new wheels."

"Not bad," said the Captain. "That'll work during the slow season. But what happens if we're really busy and the servicepeople are backed up?"

"Hadn't thought about that," said Josephine.

"Don't misunderstand. I still think it's a good concept," said the Captain, making a note. "Why don't you refine it a little more, and we'll talk again next time I visit."

Sure enough, when the Captain of Sales got back from opening yet another new MaxWheels MegaMart in downtown Thrace, Josephine and Adam had talked it over and had come up with a couple of variations on the original idea.

"If we're backed up in service and the customers don't want to wait," said Josephine, "why don't we make this offer: Buy the wheels now and we'll make an appointment with you to come to *your* place to put the wheels on your wagon at your convenience."

"Or," said Adam, "how about if we put an ad in the paper saying 'Buy your wheels by messenger! Tell us what size wheels you need and we will come to *you* and put them on your wagon.'"

"Or," said Josephine, "let it be known to people that they can drop off their chariots, ox carts, and wagons. We will then take the customers to market or to the king's palace or wherever they have to go, and we will install the wheels they need while they shop or go to court or whatever. Then we'll pick them up in a few hours at an appointed time and the work will be done."

"I love it!" said the Captain. "I love them all! Now, I am going to talk to Max and Minnie personally about them and get you the shekels you need to test them. Meanwhile, I want you to figure out exactly how they can be put into action. Next time, I'd like a plan on exactly who does what and what happens when. But we're on the way—I think we can make wheel-sales history with what this crew has come up with."

Living down by the docks of Tyre in those days was a young Greek couple whose names were Dimitri and Cassandra. Dimitri was a fisherman, and every morning at dawn he sailed away in his boat to cast his nets upon the sea. He would return sometime in the afternoon and load the catch into Cassandra's ox cart so that she could take it to the fish market and sell it to people who wanted fresh fish for dinner.

Returning home one evening, Cassandra—or Cassie, as she was known—noticed that something was wrong with the ox cart. She stopped, looked at the wheels, and discovered that one was rather worn out, while the other had developed a big crack in its wood and seemed liable to split in half sometime fairly soon.

As soon as she got home, she said to her husband, "Dimitri, the ox cart needs new wheels. Can you take a day off from fishing and get some new ones put on?"

But Dimitri said, "Take a day off? Don't you know tomorrow is the start of squid season? This year promises to offer a bumper harvest of the little buggers, and if I take a day off, Poseidon might be offended. He's the brother of Zeus, you know, and rules the oceans. I can't take that chance."

"Yeah, yeah," said his wife. "And meanwhile, what am I supposed to do about new wheels? The left one has a big crack in it!"

"Can't you take care of it tomorrow morning while I'm out in the boat?"

"But I don't know anything about wheels."

"What's to know? Just show them what you have and tell them to replace them."

"Where should I go?" asked Cassie.

"Take the cart to Imum's. They're the cheapest."

The next day, after Dimitri cast off from the dock, Cassie yoked the ox and drove to the other side of Tyre. She went right past the MaxWheels MegaMart—now painted a rich purple; she couldn't have missed it even if she'd wanted to—and she thought about stopping there. But, no, Dimitri had said to go to Imum's. So . . .

She finally found Imum's Wheel Emporium, parked the cart, and went inside. Early as it was, she happened to be the only customer, and there were four salespeople. They were a scruffy, ragged-looking bunch. One was drinking coffee and attending to some paperwork. The others were in a group by themselves, talking to one another. Cassie went over to the group of three, close enough that she figured one of them would notice her standing there. But the three salespeople just kept talking to one another.

Ten, twenty, thirty seconds went by. The three were still talking. Cassie was getting annoyed. Just as she turned to see if the coffee-drinking salesperson could help her, one of the three at last said, "Can I help you?"

"Yes, I need two new wheels for my ox cart."

"What kind?"

"Um . . . I don't know offhand."

"Well, you see, we have a lot of different wheels here. You have to know the size and type that you need."

"My cart is just outside. Couldn't you just take a look?"

Exhaling a sigh, apparently at the prospect of the effort this would take, the Imum salesguy said, "Okay, show me what you got."

They went out to the street, and the Imum guy, after examining the old wheels on the ox cart, said, "Wow."

"What's wrong?"

"These are pretty ancient. I don't know if we even carry this kind anymore. Lemme go check."

He went off into the bowels of the store and was gone for ten minutes or so, long enough that Cassie was getting impatient. She began to wonder if the guy had forgotten about her—and indeed he had. A minute later he came up the aisle with another customer.

He was about to walk past when Cassie said, "Excuse me, what about my wheels?"

The Imum guy suddenly recognized her and said, "Oh. Sorry. I thought you left."

"No, I was waiting. I need two wheels, remember?"

"Right. I checked. They're nineteen shekels a wheel."

"Fine. How soon can you have them put on my cart?"

"Well, it'll be a while. We don't have your kind in stock. But you could order them."

"How long would that take?"

"I'd say about three weeks."

"Look, I need some wheels today!" said Cassie.

The second customer now was looking at the Imum guy, and the Imum guy began looking around. "Hey, Cosmo! Can you help this lady?"

Cosmo began strolling in their direction. "What's she need?"

"Ox carts. Solid core. Three-cubit diameter."

Cosmo looked at Cassie. "I don't know if we carry those. Lemme check."

"No! *He* already checked! *You don't have them!* Just sell me some other kind of wheels that will fit my ox cart!"

Cosmo blinked. "Um, okay. Lemme check."

He, too, went back into the bowels of the store, and when he returned he said, "I don't have any three-cubits that'll fit you. But I got some four-cubits on special that I think will work."

"Okay, show me."

He took Cassie into the racks filled floor to ceiling with wheels and, after some searching, pointed out the two he was recommending. They were orange.

"Don't you have these in another color?" Cassie asked.

"Um, lemme check."

"No, just forget it. I need to get going. How much do they cost?"

"Twenty-nine shekels each. Plus tax. Plus mounting charges. Plus grease."

Cassie thought this sounded kind of pricey.

"They're, you know, heavy-duty," added Cosmo. Then he winked at her and said, "Hey, you'll be ridin' high with these babies."

"Okay, okay," Cassie said, rolling her eyes, "just get them on my cart."

Two hours later she was still waiting—and she was worrying, too. If she wasn't back at the dock when Dimitri came in with the boat, they could miss the best hours of the fish market. Then they'd likely be stuck with a boatload of smelly, rotten squid.

Meanwhile, Cosmo and the other salespeople had either forgotten about her or were ignoring her. They were off to one side, telling jokes to one another. Her only consolation was that other customers who came in got the same quality of service that she had received. At least it wasn't personal.

Finally, her ox cart—with its new, huge, orange wheels—was ready. Cassie paid the bill (seventy-two shekels total, after all the added charges) and got in. Even the ox seemed impatient to get going.

But she had barely traveled a city block when she heard a scraping sound. As she looked down, she saw that the new wheels were rubbing against the sides of the cart. Ready to explode, she got the ox to turn the cart around and went back.

The giant, axle-grease-stained guy who put the wheels on examined at the problem and said, "Yep."

"What do you mean, 'Yep'?"

"With those wheels, you really need a new axle."

"And why is that?"

"Well, those wheels are bigger, but they're also wider. You need a longer axle to move them farther out from the sides of the cart."

"How much is *that* going to cost?"

"I dunno. Lemme go get a salesguy."

A few minutes later, someone new appeared. His name tag read HI, MY NAME IS THEO. "Can I help you?"

"What happened to what's-his-name . . . Cosmo?"

"He's on break."

"Oh, well, I wouldn't want to disturb him. Look, Son of Cyclops over there says I need a new axle because of these wheels you people sold me. Nobody told me that."

Theo shrugged. "So . . . do you want a new axle or what?"

"I would like a price on a new axle," said Cassie, struggling to say it calmly.

"Okay. Lemme check."

Days later (or so it seemed), Theo returned. "That new axle you wanted? It goes for a hundred and thirty-four shekels. Plus labor. Plus tax. Plus grease."

Cassie's jaw dropped. "You're kidding."

"Ah, no, that's the price. You want us to order that for you?"

"You don't even have it in stock?"

"No, but we can get it."

"Yeah, three weeks from now," said Cassie.

"Well, I'd say four weeks, just to be safe."

"That's *it!*" Cassie shrieked. "I want those ugly orange wheels taken *off* my ox cart, I want my old wheels put back on, and I want my money back!"

Theo and the grease-stained giant exchanged a glance. "Um, I don't know if we can do that, ma'am."

"Why not?"

"You already drove on those wheels."

"So? I only went a block from the store!"

"Yeah, but they're considered used now."

"Get the manager! I demand to speak to a manager!"

"I think she's on break."

"Get her anyway!"

The Imum Wheel Emporium manager, having already been briefed on the situation by Theo, came out shaking her head. "I'm sorry, ma'am, but our policy is not to accept wheels for return once they've been driven on."

"Oh? Well, let me tell you about *my* policy. My husband is a tough, mean Greek fisherman, and if you don't take these wheels back and return my money, I'm going to have him come up here and make you eat raw squid until you puke!"

An hour later, Cassie had her old wheels and her money back. Not that she was satisfied. Not that she felt she had won. On the contrary, she had *not* solved her problem, and she just kept on hoping that the cart with its cracked wheel could make it back to the dock in time to meet Dimitri. She was worn out from fighting with the Imum people, and might have been crying if she hadn't still been so mad.

Out of the corner of her eye, she saw something big and purple: the MaxWheels MegaMart.

From the length of the shadows on the street, she guesstimated the time and concluded that she might still have an hour, more or less, before her husband sailed home with the day's catch.

On impulse, she turned the ox and parked the cart in front of the big purple store.

Going inside, she was not feeling optimistic. If a wheel was a wheel was a wheel, then a wheel store was a wheel store, right?

Her flimsy hopes fell and her defenses rose when she immediately saw two salespeople (Josephine and Tom, as it happened) standing near the door talking to each other. Cassie was expecting to be ignored—but the two members of the sales crew stopped their conversation mid-sentence when they saw her, and both turned to greet her.

"Hi, how's it going today?" asked Josephine.

"You don't want to know," said Cassie.

"Oh, my. One of those days, huh?"

"Yes. Look, I need two wheels for my ox cart, and I do not have a lot of time."

"No problem," said Josephine. "I'll hurry. Your cart is outside? Let's have a look."

When the two women got to the cart, Josephine noticed the cracked wheel right away.

> ## Minnie's Notes . . .
>
> From the customer's point of view, being taken care of is called "service." From the seller's point of view, it's "salesmanship."

"Wow, that's a bad one."

"You're telling me," said Cassie.

By now, of course, Josey—as Josephine liked to be called—had noticed an attitude on the part of Cassie. But rather than allow herself to become defensive, she went back to what she had learned from the Captain's training and tried to empathize with the woman.

"This must have been worrying the heck out of you," said Josey.

"Yes, it has been," Cassie allowed.

"Well, you don't have to worry anymore. We'll take care of you."

Cassie, however, was still suspicious. "What if you don't have them in stock?"

"Let's go check right now. If we don't, I think we can find one of our spoked wheels that will fit. And if worse comes to worst, I'll

have someone drive nails into that cracked one to hold it together while we order the new wheels."

"But that'll take three or four weeks, won't it?"

"No, that was last year. We've been working with our warehouses, and now it takes only three or four days," said Josey.

"Oh. Well, that's not so bad."

"Hey, we'll do anything we can do to shorten a customer's wait.
After all, everybody has better things to do than shop for wheels."

Almost in spite of herself, Cassie began feeling better. Here, finally, was someone who responded to her needs and respected her
time.

They went into the racks of wheels, past all the different
wagon wheels and chariot wheels, and into the ox cart wheels.

"Here, we've got 'em," said Josey, pulling out two that would fit
Cassie's cart. "Would you like these in natural beige or one of our
other colors?"

"You mean I have a choice?"

"Sure. We've got green, red, yellow, and blue."

"I like the blue. It's my favorite color," bubbled Cassie. "It always
reminds me of the sea. My husband is a fisherman, you know."

"Really? My brother is a fisherman, too," said Josey, rolling two
blue ox cart wheels down the aisle. "Today's the start of squid season, isn't it?"

"Yes, Dimitri will be back with a boatload full of them. What's
the name of your brother's boat?"

And on they chatted—until Cassie remembered she should
probably ask the price.

"Let me check," said Josey.

Cassie's face clouded, because she expected Josey to go off
someplace to look up the price. Instead, Josey pulled out a card
with all the prices listed.

"Let's see. Twenty-one shekels a wheel, plus tax. And I assume
you want them put on your ox cart?"

"Well . . . yes."

"That's three shekels per wheel."

"What about grease?"

"We don't charge for grease," said Josey. "Grease is on the house."

Cassie bit her lip. Imum had had wanted nineteen a wheel (if she had been willing to wait three weeks), but had charged her four shekels a wheel to put them on, plus one shekel for the grease. So it was the same price.

"Fine," said Cassie, "but I really don't have a lot of time. I have to meet Dimitri at the dock."

"Our policy is that if it takes more than an hour, the service is free."

"That's not the point. I *have* to be there when the catch arrives."

"Let me see what I can do. If it's going to take too long, I'll have someone do a temporary fix on the cracked wheel and we'll bring the new ones to you tomorrow morning and put them on at your house."

"That's . . . excellent! Thank you so much."

In fact, Cassie was on her way half an hour later, rolling along on new blue wheels. She was satisfied. She was even happy. And yet she wanted to kick herself.

Here I went all the way across town, she was thinking, *put up with those idiots at Imum, had to make an ugly scene to get my money back, when I could have just stopped and got MaxWheels—for the same price!*

She got to the dock just as Dimitri was tying up the boat.

"Hey, look at those nice new wheels," he said. "Did you go to Imum like I told you?"

Then he noticed the way his wife was looking at him.

"Huh? Did I say something wrong? What?"

But not all customers were as nice as Cassie. Indeed, we tend to forget that in the olden days of yore customers often behaved even more horribly than they do now.

There were some customers back in Max's time (chariot drivers, in particular) who when sold a product that was anything less than perfection would come back armed with horsewhips, javelins, swords—or sometimes all three.

On those occasions, it was certainly unpleasant, not to say unhealthy, to be a salesperson. Yet by training his sales crew, the Captain taught them not only to stop dreading irate customers, but actually to look forward to the challenge of handling them. Indeed, this could be great sport if one possessed the right skills and attitudes.

One afternoon, at a particularly busy time in the MaxWheels MegaMart, in came an ogre. He was fat, sweaty, stinky, and huge. He also had the wild of eyes of those gone berserk—and a big club that he began beating on the floor so as to get some attention.

"Well, I'm behind in the points," Tom said to Adam. "I'll take this one."

As Tom went over to deal with the ogre, a customer standing next to Adam asked, "What did he mean, he was 'behind in the points'?"

"Oh, nothing," said Adam. "Just a little game we play."

Tom approached the ogre and said, "How are you doing today?"

"Grraagghh!" said the ogre.

"What's the problem?"

"You sold me two #!^&* wheels for my chariot yesterday and they're !#*&^() junk! I took the *#^+s home, put them on, and when I went for a drive, those #!^&* wheels *wobbled!*"

"Gee, I'm sorry you're having trouble. Let's go take a look. Maybe we can figure out what's wrong."

They went out to the street, and Tom took a look at the ogre's chariot. Within a minute he had determined that the wheel hubs weren't on tight enough.

It was a simple fix, and since service was very busy that day, Tom said, "Let me get some tools and I'll take care of it for you."

He went and borrowed a wrench, tightened the hubs, then had the ogre take him for a ride around the block to make sure the trouble was really taken care of—which it was.

Back in front of the MegaMart, the ogre asked, "How much do I owe you?"

"Nothing. Don't worry about it."

Very pleased, the ogre cracked a smile. "Thanks! Have a nice day."

"You too, sir."

Tom went back inside and asked Adam, "How'd I do?"

"Pretty good," said Adam, tallying the score. "Let's see. The club and profanity he was using—right off, that doubles your score for dealing with him. You were calm, showed you were sincere, indicated you were going to do your best to solve his problem—that's four hundred points. You figured out his problem and fixed it yourself, so that's another two hundred. And you got an ogre to smile before he left, which is a two-hundred-point bonus. Looks like you're in the lead again."

"Excuse me," said the customer, "I couldn't help but overhear. You guys do that kind of thing for fun?"

"Yeah," said Tom, "and they pay us, too!"

Now, you might wonder, "Games? In the *workplace*? Wouldn't the Captain crack down on such behavior?"

No, on the contrary, the Captain encouraged games, even sponsored them—provided that they were the right kind. Games helped members of the crew focus their energies in ways that would improve their skills and improve customer service. They fostered a competitive spirit among the crew, yet they also helped pass the time—and, amazingly enough, games could sometimes even make work seem like fun.

There were real rewards for playing the games, too. Winning, or sometimes just improving substantially, could mean a few extra shekels in your paycheck. And there was praise and recognition and a semiannual awards dinner that the Captain hosted to honor crew members who had done well. Of course, the rewards flowed the other way, too.

For lo and behold, the best trade journal in the ancient wheel business, *Wheel World,* conducted a survey on customer satisfaction—and the MaxWheels MegaMarts won first place.

As part of the special issue *Wheel World* was doing to publish the results of the survey, its editors sent a reporter to the MaxWheels MegaMart store in Tyre, where the reporter interviewed the crew. Here is an excerpt:

> *Wheel World:* What's it like to have a sales job here at the MegaMart?
> *Josey:* It's work, but it's also a lot of fun.
> *WW:* Fun? Really?
> *Josey:* Yes, really!
> *WW:* Why?
> *Josey:* Well . . . I guess it's because there's always something going on.
> *WW:* Like what?
> *Adam:* You know, every couple of weeks, at the end of the day, we send out for figs and camel fritters, and we'll sit around and talk about how the MegaMart is doing and what we might be doing a little better—but after we've talked shop, we just have a good time.
> *WW:* So you like each other?
> *Sarah:* Sure. Everybody who works here is good people. You know, except for Tom.
> *Tom:* Hey!
> *Sarah:* All right, even Tom is okay. But seriously, everybody helps each other out, and we all try hard to make sure people who come into this place walk out with good experiences.
> *WW:* But, aside from free camel fritters once a week, what's in it for you? Is it the money?

Tom: The money here is decent. You know, it could always be more. But really, it's the people. This store in particular has got a great crew. And we're always challenging each other.

WW: Like how?

Josey: Oh, you know, you'll see a customer with a rotten attitude come in, and I'll say to Sarah, "I'll bet you a shekel I can make this guy lighten up and smile before he leaves."

Sarah: And I'll do the same thing. I think we've been trading the same shekel back and forth for the past couple of months.

Adam: The whole point is that it keeps things from getting dull.

Tom: Not only that, but with if we get great customer satisfaction ratings, we can win great prizes.

WW: What kind of prizes?

Adam: Like a trip to Athens.

Josey: Yeah, it's terrific! Because this MegaMart took top honors in the customer satisfaction ratings, the Captain is going to bring in people from other MegaMarts to work for us while we—and our wives and husbands—all take a trireme to Athens!

Sarah: Personally, I'm really excited. I've never seen the Parthenon before.

WW: Not many have. The Athenians just finished it.

Tom: But even if we don't win the big prizes, there are lots of little things. Like, if I solve a problem for somebody, or if I go out of my way to make something better for a customer, I know that somebody is probably going to notice it—aside from the customer.

Josey: Right, and that's a heck of a lot better than somebody NOT noticing—not caring whether or not you help people.

Sarah: Honestly, it's a great place to work.

And the four crew members were sincere in what they said. Nobody doubted that. What few outside of Max's Wheel Company comprehended was how the Captain was able to keep his crew so "up"—and, moreover, how he managed to do it on a regular, month-after-month basis. It was a mystery.

You see, with any group, you will generally tend to find a small minority who will outperform the others. (And, conversely, you will also find a minority who will underperform.) Typically, the ratio is that one or two out of ten will prove to be stars, and one or two out of ten will be duds.

What the Captain of Sales did was elevate the performance of the entire crew to a new standard—so that the stars were superb, the average crew members were terrific, and the duds (if they lasted) were at least adequate.

He did this through a combination of measures, most of them mentioned afore: careful selection and hiring, good training (and not just once, but ongoing), and the special magic of empowerment.

But beyond all of those was a continuous effort to find and use fresh, low-cost, or no-cost incentives that would keep the naturally boring and humdrum job of selling wheels from becoming boring and humdrum.

The Captain was always paying attention to the state of the crew. He spent a lot of time traveling to the MegaMarts in his fleet, or, if he couldn't spare the time, he would have his most trusted lieutenants do it. How was each crew's morale? Which incentives were working? Which were just a waste of time and shekels? How could this system or that be made to work just a little bit better? He was always asking those kinds of questions—and always listening to others for the answers.

What the Captain understood better than anyone was what you could and could not expect of a sales crew. At the core, the crew was made up of normal people—mostly young—who would never possess the work ethic of a Ben, could never fathom the special knowledge of a Toby, and had nowhere near the ambition or the charm of a Cassius. Fundamentally, these were people who just wanted to have a nice job, work their hours in the store, and go home at night. Glorious careers didn't interest them. Money alone didn't motivate them. If you wanted something special from them, then you had to keep being creative.

That was the Captain's big secret. That was how he was able to raise the performance not just of a few individuals, but of the entire organization—and do it not just one year, but year after year.

Well, Imum tried to copy some of the Captain's ideas, but he never really got them right. He offered free vacations—but only to the top-performing salespeople, and he tied the incentive to sales rather than customer satisfaction.

Ozzie's Insights . . .

Top Characteristics of a World Class Sales Crew

- A leader who repeatedly drives home the need to "make the customer happy."
- Highly efficient systems for servicing customers—yet also an avoidance of stiff formality in policies; an organizational willingness to bend the rules when warranted to keep individual customers happy.
- Compensation often is based in part on some measurement of customer satisfaction.
- Ongoing training programs to develop skills and keep the crew up to date with respect to systems and product knowledge.
- A management effort to make the company a great place to work. Lots of cheerleading. A recognition that crew salespeople are not self-starting and require strong leadership to perform well.
- Common liabilities: shallow technical understanding; an inability to deal with anything for which a corporate system has not been devised.

As a result, there were an unscrupulous few who tried every underhanded trick they could think of—just to win the vacation. In the end, Imum paid for free vacations for a few, but that neither helped Imum's customers nor boosted performance of the organization as a whole. In fact, the majority of salespeople—who did not win anything—were kind of upset. Morale sank ever lower—and so, in turn, did Imum's share of the wheel market.

After all, if you were living in those times, where would you buy your wheels? Would you always, always, always go for the lowest price? Even if it meant doing so was likely going to ruin your day? Or would you pay an extra shekel or two and be pretty well assured that you were going to be able to leave the store in a reasonably good mood?

In the long run, there were millions of wheel customers who were like Cassie and Dimitri—who always went back to the MaxWheels MegaMart whenever they needed new wheels for the ox cart.

Month after month, those few extra shekels per wheel began to add up. Before long, Max's Wheel Company was the most profitable in the industry. Wisely, Max reinvested a portion of the profits to gain greater efficiency in the company, and in a matter of a few years, customers didn't have to choose between a low price and great service. They could have both.

Max's company went from third in wheel sales and first in customer satisfaction to first in satisfaction *and* sales, offering a lower price than Imum could ever hope to match.

Finally, it happened. The rumors had been flying for weeks, first as whispers. Imum's suppliers were grumbling about late payments from the wheel-making giant. Then came word that Lebanese Lumber, who sold the wood for wheels to Imum, had stopped extending credit; for Imum's factory to get a delivery of wood, there had to be a bag of shekels waiting for L.L.'s wagon driver.

Next came the ads and banners proclaiming wheel sales offering unheard-of discounts. For a while, Minnie and Max were worried. How could Imum cut prices so low and still stay in business? The answer was soon forthcoming.

What began as whispers and grumbles ended suddenly in head-lines:

IMUM BANKRUPT!
DOZENS OF WHEEL EMPORIUMS TO CLOSE!
HUNDREDS OF TERRIBLE SALESPEOPLE
MUST FIND NEW JOBS!

The messenger arrived as Max was reading the story.

"What's this?" he asked.

"A message from Imum."

Max opened the note, and this is how it read:

Dear Max,

We have been business rivals for many years. Many are the occasions when I thought we had you beat, when I thought perhaps you might be the one to send a message such as this. However, those days are now behind us.

Would you please honor me with your presence in a meet-ing at your earliest convenience? I have a proposal that might be of interest and considerable profit to you.

Sincerely,

Imum

A few hours later, Max and Imum were sitting across a table from each other.

"What's on your mind?" asked Max.

"Things haven't worked out the way I'd planned," said Imum.

"Yes, I've heard."

"How would you like to buy Imum Industries?"

Though Max had kind of expected that this might be the purpose of the meeting, the reality of the offer stunned him.

At last, he said to Imum, "All right, let me see your books."

He studied Imum's accounting ledgers for an hour or two, then closed the leather-bound tomes with a thump and said, "I'll offer you fifty million shekels for the works."

"I need a hundred million."

"Seventy-five," Max returned. "That's my best offer."

Imum swallowed. "I'll take it. On one condition . . ."

An hour later, Max walked out of the meeting with a smile on his face. He was going to be president and CEO of a company almost twice as large as the one he had managed when he got up that morning: the MaxImum Wheel Corporation.

That had been Imum's one condition to the deal, that his name be attached to the new company.

Max didn't care. He thought that "MaxImum" had nice ring to it. More important, he would be the head of the largest wheel company in the world, a company that would dominate the market.

Euphoric, he stepped off the curb into the street—whereupon he was immediately run over by a speeding chariot.

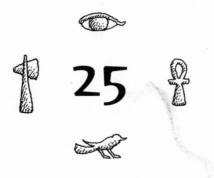

25

Yet Max survived.

Just barely. For a year, he hovered at Death's Door—then took another year to fully regain his health.

At last, he felt well enough to get out of bed one morning, get dressed, and sit at the kitchen table for breakfast.

"Here's a cup of coffee, dear," said his wife. "Would you like to read the morning paper?"

"Sure! Haven't seen a paper in two years! Got a lot of catching up to do."

He sipped his coffee and turned to the financial pages—and nearly had a heart attack.

"*What?* Has the market gone crazy?" he thundered.

"What, the wheel market?"

"No, the stock market!"

"Well, yes, dear . . . it's up five thousand points since you first went into your coma."

"Then what's happened to the price of shares in MaxImum Wheel?"

"Oh, they were pushing a hundred shekels a share for a while, just after the merger," said Minnie.

"Then why were they down to thirty-three and an eighth at yesterday's close?"

"They tanked, dear."

"Why?"

"All the shekel sages downgraded us. MaxImum was dropped from the Pharaoh's Phavorite Picks List. Everybody rates our stock as either a Hold or a Sell."

"How could this happen?"

"I don't know," said Minnie. "Something about how our price-earnings multiple wasn't justified by future-earnings estimates. So pension funds from Babylon to Carthage started puking our shares, sending the share price plummeting."

"Oh." Max thought for a moment. "But aren't we still selling wheels?"

"Yes, by the billions. But we can't seem to earn much in the way of profits. Revenues have been flat, and margins are razor thin."

Max folded the paper and slapped it down onto the table.

"Minnie, grab your cloak. We're going to the office."

And what an office it had become. Max's jaw dropped the moment he saw it. There were dozens of fat marble columns, and gilded statues, and fountains, and a cadre of uniformed trumpeters to herald the arrival of executives and distinguished visitors.

Carved into the marble above the columns were the words:

MAXIMUM WHEEL CORPORATION
WORLD HEADQUARTERS
Excellence in Everything

The drivers of the golden carriage that had brought Max and Minnie halted right in front of the grand entrance, with its marble steps rising to the enormous bronze doors that were adorned with sculpted depictions of Great Moments in Wheel History.

Max and Minnie alighted from the carriage—and were nearly flattened by the blare of the trumpets.

"Whose idea was all this?" Max asked.

"Ed. It was Ed's idea."

"Ed? Who's Ed?"

"Ed the Effusive. We hired him shortly after your accident," said Minnie. "I mean, I had never managed a corporation the size of MaxImum before. I had to get *somebody*, and Ed was a vice president at Trans-Asiatic Caravan Corporation."

"Isn't that the company that imported all those Chinese wheel clones that nearly drove us under?"

"Yes, but I just thought . . . oh, here comes Ed now!"

Flying down the steps came a handsome, grinning man with his brilliant white toga fluttering behind him and his arms spread wide in greeting.

"Max! What a surprise! You've returned! How fabulous!" He embraced Max, kissed him on both cheeks, and asked, "How are you feeling? Are you sure you're up to this?"

"Oh, yes. I'm fine. You're Ed, I take it?"

"We met shortly after the board of directors approved my compensation package. But you were in a coma, so I don't think you'd remember it. Please, do come in! There is so much to show you! Why don't we start with the executive dining room? I just know you'll be so excited when you see it!"

"Hold on, Ed. I think I'd rather start with what you've got carved in stone up there. 'Excellence in Everything.' What does that mean?"

"Don't you just love it? My idea. I have established as our corporate goal that we are going to be excellent in absolutely everything we do."

"Yeah? How about excellence in net income?"

"Oh. Well, we *are* working on that. I was even considering setting that as next year's big goal."

"Really? Then let me help get you off to a good start. See those trumpeters over there? Fire them."

"But, Max!"

"And that golden carriage we came in? Sell it. Get me a basic chariot—and one driver in a normal tunic will do fine."

"Oh, but, Max, the board approved golden carriages for all of the executives."

"Uh-huh. Well, I believe I'm still chairman of the board. Take all the golden carriages and put them in a warehouse. Tell the executives they can have them back when MaxImum's stock price stays above a hundred shekels a share."

"Now, Max, let's not be hasty. You have to understand that as the world's largest wheel company, we have to set the proper image."

"I totally agree. Fire the trumpeters. Put the golden carriages in storage. And let's go inside and see what the numbers look like."

For the rest of the day (except for a brief luncheon served on plates made of various precious metals in the executive dining room), Max went through the books.

Late in the afternoon, he called in Ed the Effusive.

"Ed, I appreciate your efforts these past two years. I do believe you've had good intentions. But after thinking it over for much of the afternoon, I've decided to give you some new responsibilities."

"Max, I hate to remind you, but there is the silver sails clause in my contract—"

"Oh, we'll honor the terms, of course, but should you choose to remain with us, I've decided that you should have a fresh assignment. Something commensurate with your accomplishments."

"What might that be?"

"The barbarians, Ed. I'd like you to spearhead the opening of the barbarian wheel markets. Take those folks on the other side of the Alps, those Teutonic tribes the Romans are always complaining about. Ed, they're just not buying any wheels."

"They don't have any roads."

"Ah-ha! I knew a man of your intelligence would grasp the situation right away. I want you to go north and convince those Teutons that they ought to build an autobahn. I'll bet you those people could build some pretty speedy chariots and such if they just had some roads to drive them on. And then, you see, we can sell them the wheels!"

Ed's face took on a sour look. "But . . . they're so hairy and rough!"

"I'm sure they'll appreciate someone of your fine cultural sensibilities. Now, get cracking, and once you've got that autobahn under way, you can move on to the Celts and the Danes and the Huns and—heck, you just can head on east and talk to the Mongols."

"All right. Let me start putting together my retinue. I'll need plenty of servants, and casks of the best wine for entertaining, and all of the finest amenities—"

"Fine, as long as you can do it on a thousand shekels."

"A day?"

"A year."

"You've got to be kidding! That's absurd! I won't endure such hardship! I quit!"

At this, Ed the Effusive huffed out, causing the idea of the autobahn to be lost for centuries.

Going around the corner to Minnie's office, Max told her, "I've taken care of Ed. Now, let's get down to the real problem: How do we turn this company around and get sales and earnings growing again?"

As Max knew, there were two parts to turning the situation around and making the company strong again. The first part of the solution was to cut costs: If sales stayed the same but costs went down, then obviously the company would make more money.

Of the two, that part was relatively easy—especially since the excesses of Ed the Effusive had created a lot of opportunities for scaling back the company's expenses.

But the second part of the solution was more puzzling. That was the question of how to make sales revenue grow. This was really going to be a problem, because, as Minnie explained to Max, research showed that the wheel market was going to grow only one or two percent a year.

So, unless the Pharaoh, or some other king, decided to go to war and suddenly ordered a bunch of new chariots (a prospect Max personally did not welcome), the market, in effect, was stagnant.

To make matters worse, there were not only Chinese wheels streaming into the market, but also wheels from places like India and even Siam. The civilized world was flooded with cheap wheels, and prices had never been lower.

"It's just maddening," said Minnie. "Even as efficient as we've made our factories and our distribution systems, we still can't turn out wheels any more cheaply than the Chinese or the others. Every time we lower prices, they come out with even lower ones."

There were even vendors selling wheels on the street—with literally no overhead, just a stack of wheels in the open air and enough shekels to make change. These wheels were selling for as little as two or three shekels. Of course, there was no service; buyers just picked them up, paid, and took them home.

"How are we ever going to compete when customers don't care about great service, when they're happy just to take the absolute lowest price and put the wheels on themselves?" asked Minnie.

Max stroked his chin. "I don't know." Then asked, "Don't you have any good news?"

"There are a few bright spots," his wife allowed.

She explained that Toby the Wizard was still doing a great job selling Millstone systems to granaries near and far. She and her fellow wizards sold only a few dozen a year, but MaxImum made a very good margin on those—the best of any product the company sold.

Meanwhile, Ben the Builder had done a great job developing the specialty wheel market. And though the company had at one point nearly lost Atlas Wagon as a customer, Ben's superior salesmanship and service had kept them on board. He had even managed to bring in Amalgamated Ox Cart, as well as a small piece of business with General Chariot—even though the prices Ben quoted were higher than the going commodity prices.

"But even there we have problems," said Minnie.

"Like what?"

All of MaxImum's systems those days were set up to supply the mass market through the MegaMarts. Ben had been complaining loud and long about how hard it was for him to get his orders for 10,000 or 20,000 wheels shipped on time—when the Captain's staff was sending in orders for 50,000 and 100,000 wheels.

"The trouble is," said Minnie, "we're all but giving away those lots of 100,000 wheels. We're lucky to make even half a shekel on those kinds of wheels anymore."

"Then why are we producing them?"

"I'm told that if the factory isn't running full tilt, our costs per wheel go up, and then we're sure to be priced out of the market."

"Let me see if I've got this right," said Max. "We make the most profit on the wheels we sell less of. But we're best set up to produce the kinds of wheels on which our profit is slim to none."

"That's about it," said his wife.

"Arrgh! How did things get so screwed up?"

Then Minnie had what seemed like a wonderful idea.

"You know," she said, "I still think we have the best salespeople in the business. Why don't we get Toby, Ben, and the Captain together with us in one room, and we'll have a nice lunch, then we'll pose the problem to them: How do we get sales growing again? And, you know, we could even invite Cassius the Closer—word is that he's in town again."

The more Max thought about this, the more he liked it. "Yeah! I'm sure they'll have lots of good suggestions, and afterward we can take the best of them and put them into action! Brilliant! Let's do it!"

So began what became known as the Armageddon of Sales.

They booked a room at the Camel Club and brought in the four great salespeople for the off-site, no-distractions meeting. And for lunch, the club had prepared for them the latest thing in culinary delights: the smorgasbord.

Seldom mentioned by historical scholars, the smorgasbord was introduced to the region by the ancestors of Vikings, who came down the Dnieper River and across the Black Sea to trade furs and, you know, have a little fun in the sun. Anyway, it was all the rage, and when Ed the Effusive held affairs at the Camel Club, he *always* insisted on a smorgasbord—so when the club saw that the luncheon was being hosted by the MaxImum Wheel Corporation, the kitchen staff automatically assumed a smorgasbord was called for.

And on this occasion, the club's chefs outdid themselves. The smorgasbord was huge, with all kinds of imported northern foods: everything from urns of slaw and big bowls of different salads to tubs of potatoes, buckets of sardines, platters piled with fried eggs, pots of mixed vegetables, plates of chops, heaps of steaming weenies—as well as selected Mediterranean favorites like stuffed grape leaves, pita bread, olive oil, and so on. And then there was dessert: an enormous pastry cart laden with every kind of pie from cherry to coconut goat custard.

After all of them had stuffed themselves, Max opened the discussion by explaining the quandary in which he and Minnie found themselves.

"That's why we brought all of you together," he concluded. "How can we get the sales of this once-great company of ours growing again? We would very much like to hear your thoughts on the matter."

For several seconds, everyone in the room was silent. Then Cassius the Closer spoke up.

"I can tell you exactly what's wrong," said Cassius. "And I can do it by posing a question of my own: How long has it been since this company has introduced a truly revolutionary product to the marketplace?"

Upon this opening comment, all the salespeople jumped in.

"Cassius is right," said Toby the Wizard. "If we want sales to grow, we need new, groundbreaking products—which in turn means we need to invest more in research and development."

"Now, wait a minute," said the Captain of Sales. "Revolutionary products are very risky. I say we slash the R&D budget and pump that money into advertising to build brand-name loyalty."

"Advertising? For the kinds of commodity wheels you're selling? That's just throwing money away," said Ben the Builder. "Look, the wheel market is here to stay, can we all agree on that?"

Everyone except Cassius nodded.

"We don't need to go chasing some exotic new technology that the market might not accept," Ben continued, "not when there are still billions upon billions of shekels to be made selling wheels.

"At the same time, we've got warehouses full of wheels that are no different and no better than the ones coming in from China. What we need are wheels that customers will pay a little bit extra to get. I believe that 'little bit extra' is going be the difference between profit and loss for this company. If we spend R&D money on anything, let's put it into developing new features and options that will offer a lot more value for a little bit higher price."

"You're all missing the point!" said Cassius. "Yes, the wheel is here to stay, but it's yesterday's technology! Why do you want to sell yesterday when you can sell the future?"

"Because the customer doesn't care about the future! The customer cares about today!" Ben all but shouted. "Let's forget about the future, let's put our customers first, let's build great relationships with each of them, and solve their problems of today!"

"Sure," said Toby, "today's products are fine—until somebody brings out, say, a rubber wheel and makes every wooden wheel we're selling obsolete!"

"A rubber wheel?" asked the Captain. "Never heard of such a thing. And anyway, who would want one?"

"Lots of people, if the manufacturing process could be perfected."

"Bah! Wooden wheels are practical and proven!"

"That's what everyone said about stone wheels until wooden ones came along," said Toby. "And I don't suppose any of you saw the story in the latest *Wheel Science Journal*, did you?"

"I don't have time for that blue-skies, theoretical garbage," said the Captain.

"Well, then, you missed the story about how putting a band of iron around the circumference of a wooden wheel dramatically improves both its performance and durability."

"Really? Who's the inventor?" asked Cassius.

Toby ignored him. "Listen, if somebody comes out with iron-banded wheels ahead of us, I wouldn't give this company two years."

"Hah! We're the biggest wheel company in the world!" said the Captain.

"Actually," said Ben, "I could see offering iron banding as a option in a year or two."

"A year or two might be too late!" argued Toby. "Let me go now to talk to General Chariot and propose a joint venture to develop the technology. Then we'll get a jump on everyone else."

"Hey, General Chariot is my customer," said Ben. "You don't know anybody there!"

"I don't need to! My credentials will get me in—and I'll be talking to upper management, not purchasing."

"Okay," said the Captain, "let's hold up here. Max, I don't mean any disrespect to my colleagues, but it's clear to me what the real problem with this company is: It's a question of focus."

"And what do you mean by that?" asked Minnie.

"Just that we are who we are: the MaxImum Wheel Corporation, the largest wheel company in the world. We have to do what size does best.

"I have nothing against Cassius, but visionaries often can't see reality. If we go chasing after tomorrow, we're going to miss the sales we can harvest today.

"And Millstones? Toby is very talented, a brilliant engineer, but the truth is that Millstones are a lot of dead weight on this company."

"Then why are we the most profitable?" asked Toby.

"The market for Millstones is just too small for a company this size!" said the Captain. "Let's spin off Millstones and put the proceeds toward the true purpose of this company: being the leader in low-cost, high-volume wheel sales.

"Which brings me to Ben's operation. No question that Ben treats his customers right—only he can't give that level of service to every customer . . . and I can."

"The hell you can!" said Ben. "One of your sales-crew 'kids' couldn't even make it through lunch with one of my customers!"

"Well, Ben," said the Captain, "we all know that lunch is what you do best."

"What I do best is add value to sales through my own hard work!" shouted Ben.

"Whoa! Hold it!" said Max. "Captain, if you have a point, why don't you just spit it out."

"My point is simply this: that we should eliminate or reduce all other operations to focus on the big prize—continued dominance of standard, mass-market wheel sales."

For a moment, silence.

Then Minnie said, "What, so that we can have no net income at all?"

"If we trimmed the fat, we could be profitable," said the Captain.

"Fat? You're calling ME fat?" screamed Toby. "You MegaMarts are the part that's unprofitable!"

"You want my opinion?" asked Cassius. "Say what you want about vision. As far as selling, none of you people know how to close!"

"Right, you can close, Cassius, but you can't service!" said Toby. "Or should I dredge up some of the ugly details of the Great Pyramid job?"

"One of my customers," said Ben, "wouldn't give you more than a single meeting!"

"That's all I need," said Cassius.

"Yeah, and any more, you lose the business, because you close and you're gone!"

"Wait, hold it! Calm down!" said Minnie, seeing that everyone was losing control. "Let's take it easy for a minute. Would anybody like some goat custard pie for dessert?"

"Goat custard? Never tried it, but I'm game," said Cassius.

"It's delicious. My grandmother's favorite," said Ben. "I'll have a slice."

"All right. I'd like a big piece," said the Captain.

"Just a small piece will be enough for me," said Toby, "as long as it's nice and rich."

It remains a mystery who threw the first piece. Suddenly the pie was flying everywhere but the sky.

In the aftermath of the pie fight, having sent the salespeople home to clean up, Max and Minnie sat bewildered amidst the splatters and speckles of gooey fillings and the flakes of shattered crusts.

"What a mess," Minnie complained.

"That was disgusting," said Max.

"Highly unprofessional."

"Yes, but . . . it was more fun than I've ever had at a business lunch."

A smile crossed his wife's face. "True . . . I did nail Cassius with that lemon cream." Then the smile faded. "But, Max, what are we going to do? We've got a sales force that's in chaos!"

Just then the head waiter appeared, cleared his throat, and presented the bill—the total of which included 100 shekels for miscellaneous cleaning charges. Max simply added a generous tip and signed the tab.

"Thank you, sir," said the waiter. "Will there be anything else?"

"Yes, wrap the leftovers of the smorgasbord. We'll be taking them with us."

"Oh, but, Max," said his wife, "we'll never be able to finish all that."

"They're not for us," he said. "They're for our good friend."

The next day, the two of them stood at the entrance to cave. While Max built a fire, Minnie unpacked the food, and then together they reheated everything.

When the Oracle appeared, he was overwhelmed. "Oh, my! What is all this?"

"Smorgasbord! It's the latest thing!" said Minnie.

"I hope you're hungry!" added Max.

"Well, ah . . . it's a little much," said the Oracle.

His eyes roved from the slaws and salads to the tubs of pasta, the buckets of sardines and anchovies, the piles of fried eggs, the pots of mixed vegetables, the plates of chops, the heaps of weenies, and everything else.

"Go ahead!" Max urged. "Dig right in!"

"What's the matter?" asked Minnie. "Aren't you pleased? I'm sorry there isn't any pie, but—"

"No, that's okay!" said the Oracle. "There is quite enough here, only . . . I'm just not very hungry at the moment."

"But . . . we have a big problem to discuss with you," said Minnie.

"Yes, can't you at least force down a little snack?"

"Oh, all right," said the Oracle, reaching for a plate. "Maybe some fruit."

While the Oracle nibbled on some grapes, Max and Minnie told him everything that had happened, even about the disastrous lunch that had ended in a pie fight.

Suddenly the Oracle got a certain look on his face. "Do you know why your company is in trouble? Because you've become just like this monstrosity of a smorgasbord you've offered me."

"I don't understand," said Minnie.

"Let me show you something," said the Oracle. He took a charred stick from the remains of the fire and drew the outlines of four animals on the wall of the cave.

"Now," he asked, pointing to the first animal, "do you recognize this shape?"

"It looks like a bird," said Max.

"Very good! In fact, though I'm not much of an artist, it's supposed to be a falcon. What are the others?"

"The next one is a camel," said Minnie.

"Good."

"Next is a horse."

"And the last?"

"An elephant," said Max.

"Right you are. Tell me now, aside from all being members of the animal kingdom, what do they have in common?"

Max and Minnie thought for a minute, but gave up.

"They can all do a job for us," said the Oracle. "Take the falcon, for example. If we train the falcon and treat it well, it will fly off, hunt small game, and return with dinner."

"True," said Minnie.

"Falcons are magnificent in flight and are highly prized by aristocrats—but let's say you have a chariot and you need an animal to pull it. Would you try to harness the falcon to the chariot?"

"No, I'd use the horse," said Max.

"Exactly! By the same token, would you try to train the horse to fly?"

"Of course not."

"No, the horse is strong and fast, and capable of many tasks, but it won't fly. Nor is it good for all jobs. Let's say you have to move an extremely heavy load—a big pile of logs or heavy stones—and you could use only one animal to get the job done. Would you choose the horse?"

"I'd probably pick the elephant," said Minnie.

"Right. For moving a mass of bulky, heavy materials, the elephant, if it's well trained, would be the most efficient choice. But suppose you had to get to the other side of the Sahara, would you pick the elephant to get you there?"

"No, the camel," said Minnie.

"Yes, obviously. Both the horse and the elephant would likely die in the middle of the desert and leave you stranded. But the camel could make the journey because of its highly specialized capabilities. Camels are not as generally useful as horses or as strong as elephants. They can be headstrong, stubborn, and even arrogant. On the other hand, if you need to move goods across vast, dry areas, you get a camel."

"Okay, what are you driving at?" asked Max.

"Look," said the Oracle, "you have four excellent salespeople at your disposal. But each is a different animal; each is most suitable for a job that matches its nature.

"Cassius is your falcon—a bit exotic, independent, soaring off into the blue sky and bringing back the prize, so long as you feed him well when he returns.

"Toby is your camel—also a bit exotic, though not very glamorous; highly specialized, and amazingly capable in certain harsh environments.

"Ben is your horse—charging to the rescue, but also terrific at daily, mundane tasks like pulling a wagon.

"And the Captain and his crew are the elephant—the strongest of all the animals, capable of moving a lot of mass," said the Oracle. "Now think about this: Would you *ever* try to harness all these animals together at the same time?"

"You mean try to get them all to pull together? No," said Max.

"It likely wouldn't work very well," said Minnie, "and it might even turn out to be a disaster."

"Right. And yet that is what you are expecting of them right now. You have one company, but you're trying to harness all four of these great creatures at the same time. It will not work."

Max sighed. "Okay, but can't we use all four if we don't try to harness them into one team?"

The Oracle thought for a moment. Then he took a candle from one of the many pockets of his robe. He lit the candle, then picked up an orange from the smorgasbord spread, and said, "Come with me."

The Oracle then took Max and Minnie back into the darkest reaches of the cave, where it was completely black except for the light of the candle. Now, the Oracle held up the orange next to the small flame.

"Let's say this candle is your company," he said, "and this orange is the total market for wheels. The rays of the candle are your company's ability to serve that market. How much of the orange can one candle illuminate?"

"Half," said Minnie.

"Exactly right. And with one company, that is the maximum you should try to manage," said the Oracle. "Now the question is, which half do you want?"

◆   ◆   ◆

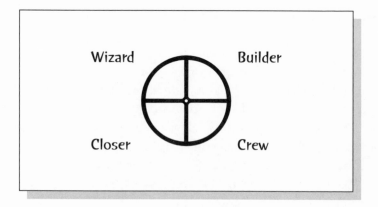

He brought them back to the front of the cave and picked up the charred stick again.

He drew a picture of a wheel on the wall of the cave, saying, "Let's say this represents the whole wheel market."

Then he drew four spokes, quartering the wheel, and he labeled each quarter according to the four types of selling.

"Let me say first," said the Oracle, "that the vast majority of businesses out there operate in only one quarter of the total market—and sometimes in just a tiny sliver. That's fine, because that's really all they competently can manage, and the best companies focus on what they do best.

"Your company, however, has been extraordinarily successful—in part, perhaps, because of the wise advice you've received—and because of that success you are now a big company. You can, therefore, take on more than one segment of the market. But if you are smart, you will abide by the Rule of Half.

"Look, if you feel your company will do best by being small, nimble, entrepreneurial, and technically progressive—always looking for the next wave—then the best marketing and sales strategy is to adopt a closer-wizard style.

"Do you want high-margin, profitable growth? Then the right combination is a wizard-builder style. You take emerging new technologies, you develop them using the wizard style of selling until they become accepted, then you turn them over to builders, who handle them until they are so standardized that you find you're competing on price and convenience—at which point you sell off those businesses and reinvest the capital in yet another emerging technology.

"Or maybe you want the company to be huge and dominant. Your goal here is slow, steady, predictable growth. In that case, you'll want a builder-crew sales strategy. You don't develop new technology, but as soon as it's clearly accepted by most of the market, you acquire it through mergers, buyouts, and takeovers. Your builders take the lead, but as competition standardizes options and puts on price pressure, you phase in a captain-and-crew style—and manage it in that fashion until the technology is obsolete.

"There you have it," concluded the Oracle. "Look at your company, figure out your true strengths, and make your choice. But be aware that if you choose to keep two selling styles, you will have a primary and a secondary market. If you have a secondary market, you can expect it to be half as profitable as your primary market. And if you choose to stay in three, expect the third to lose money."

Then Max, who had been stroking his chin, deep in thought, for the past minute or two, finally said, "I just don't get it. Why can't we use all four—as long as we keep them separate?"

"Simply put," said the Oracle, "it's because no one company

Max's Maxim

No Company Can Be All Things to All Customers. Therefore, Choose the Customers for Whom You Can Deliver the Most Value!

can be all things to all customers. You learned that in your lun-cheon: the drives and needs of the salespeople, the markets, and the customers create too many conflicts. You can't possibly man-age that kind of chaos. Take either your quarter or your half of the wheel universe and be the leader in those segments. My best to you . . . and good luck."

And with that the Oracle faded back into the darkness.

"The Captain is here to see you."

Minnie thanked her assistant, then she and Max rose in greeting.

"Have a seat, Captain. We'd like to have a talk with you."

"What's on your minds?"

"Captain, you've done an admirable job, and the MaxImum Wheel Corporation can't thank you enough."

"Oh, well, you know . . . thanks. All along, I just did what I thought best."

"But in spite of your best efforts and those of the crew, Max and I have come to the conclusion that it's time to abandon ship."

"Excuse me?"

"You're a tremendous sales manager," said Max, "perhaps the best there is in these ancient times of ours."

"And the crew is second to none," added Minnie, "as the surveys year after year have shown."

"The reality, Captain, is that we cannot compete . . . no, that's not quite accurate. The fact is that we do not *want* to compete, given current prices, at the commodity end of the wheel market—not when there are other, more promising opportunities we wish to pursue."

"On the other hand," said Minnie, "if you accept our offer, you'll have a new title, lots more responsibility, and the compensation to go with them."

"Offer? New title? Pardon me, but are you firing me or giving me a promotion?"

"Both," said Minnie. "We'd like you to become president and CEO of MegaMarts Unlimited."

"We've decided to spin off the MegaMart chain into a separate company. You'll have your own show, Captain."

"And we," said Minnie, "will gain lots of new capital that we can reinvest in building dominance in what we see as our core businesses."

"Besides," added Max, "without the politics of MaxImum holding you down, you'll be able to sell any wheels you wish to carry—Chinese, Indian, Roman, as well as MaxWheels . . . or whatever customers want."

"I like it!" said the Captain.

"Good," said Max. "Well, you've got a lot of work to do, and you'd best get to it. We'll be talking every day or two about bringing this off. Good luck with your new command."

"Thank you," said the Captain. "Thank you so much!"

After he had left, Max said to Minnie, "I think that went well. Let's talk to the others."

"Hello, Ben. Have a seat."

"Why the long face?" Minnie asked him.

"I just passed the Captain of Sales in the hallway on his way out," said Ben. "He looked so pleased that . . . well, I figure this meeting isn't going to have much good news for me."

"Actually, we *have* made some important decisions."

"One of them," said Max, "is that your builder group is to going to be the core of this company's future."

Ben sat up straight, hardly able to believe what he had just been told. "Could you say that again?"

"You heard right. You and your builders are going to be at the center of the way we do business in the future."

"Now, we have a question for you," said Minnie.

"Ben, if I'm correct in my hunches, you wouldn't want the top management spot in this company even if we offered it to you, right?"

"Well, I . . . ah, that is . . . let's put it this way: It's always flattering to be asked. But to tell you the truth, and I mean no disrespect here, I really feel that management is boring, and sales is where the action is."

"Say no more," said Max. "That's fine. We thought that's pretty much how you would feel about it."

"But we're going to give you a promotion anyway," said Minnie. "We're going to make you a vice president. You'll still have ongoing contact with our best and biggest accounts. Your main responsibility, though, will be continually looking for ways your salespeople can add value for our customers."

"That's . . . terrific! Thank you!"

"I'll warn you," said Max, "you won't be able to rest on your laurels. We'll be looking to you to bring in new accounts—and you're soon going to have some new products to sell."

"No problem. What new products do you have in mind?"

"Why don't you come with us."

The three of them strolled through the MaxImum Building's labyrinth of marble halls, arriving finally at a heavy iron door guarded by sentries with spears. The sentries stepped aside as the party approached, and Max opened the door and led the way inside.

They entered a cavernous room with all manner of wizards, sorcerers, and their assistants laboring over various arcane contraptions and laboratory apparatus. Among them was Toby.

She was standing near a strange device, something Ben had never seen before.

"What the heck is that?" Ben asked, peering over her shoulder.

"That," said Max, "is our future—part of it, at least."

"It looks like two wheels with teeth around their edges."

"And that's what it is," said Toby, "except that we call them 'gears.' Allow me to demonstrate."

She turned a crank attached to the bigger of the two gears, and as the gear turned, so did the smaller one as its teeth engaged those of the larger.

"See," said Toby, "turning one gear makes the other one move. But you'll notice that the smaller gear rotates much faster than the larger one. What this means, simply, is that I can use torque to create speed."

"Huh," said Ben. "But what would you use these gears to do?"

"Take a look at this," said Max, turning to another device nearby. "The Grinding Wheel. It's one of our old stone wheels that's turned by a crank-and-gear arrangement. You turn the crank, the gears turn the stone, and you can use it to sharpen everything from swords to scissors."

"This is just the beginning," said Toby. "Gears can be used, say, to drive pairs of rollers to make flat sheets of metal. . . . Or they'll be used in lathes or different kinds of mills. In fact, we think that gears will be essential components in many useful gadgets called 'machines' that can produce all kinds of products we can't even imagine today."

"Well, I'll be . . ." said Ben.

"But we're not just betting our future on the gear," said Max. "Show him the other things we've got going."

"Check this out," said Toby. "This is what we call the 'pulley.' We can use pulleys in a system called a 'Block and Tackle' to raise heavy stuff with less effort than it would otherwise require."

"Yeah, like sailors could use this kind of thing to raise the heavy sails on a boat," said Max.

"This is my favorite," said Minnie, "the Water Wheel."

She showed Ben a working model of the wheel that would be used to convert the weight of water into turning motion.

"Amazing," said Ben.

"All of this right now is high technology," Max explained. "As it becomes practical to do so, it will be the job of our wizards to sell this technology as advanced, state-of-the-art systems. However, even though we'll expect them to be profitable, their role in our strategy is really to be the avant-garde to the main force—which will be you and your builders. As these technologies become standardized into accepted, reproducible products, that's when your builders will come in. The builders will take the technologies with the most commercial potential and sell them to the most desirable customers. You with me?"

"Sure," said Ben.

"Eventually, some of these products will become so standardized, so simplistic, and so easily produced that they will become commodities. At that point, we will sell those product lines to other businesses in a position to profit best from commodities. By staying in higher-profit product lines, we'll be able to invest in R&D here in the lab to keep on developing new technologies and new products."

"Wow. This sounds like a cycle we could repeat over and over—endlessly!"

"That is the basic idea, yes."

"I'm excited!"

"Good," said Max. "So are we. Now, there is just one more thing we need to discuss. Toby . . ."

"Yes?"

"You've done a tremendous job selling Millstones and other wheel systems over the years. But Minnie and I would like you to train a replacement for those duties."

"Why is that?"

"Because . . . well, being run over by a speeding chariot made me realize that I'm not getting any younger. I'd like for Minnie and I to retire. When we do, I want you to become president and CEO of MaxImum. We ran the idea past Ben, but the truth is that sales, not management, is in his blood. Besides, given the new strategy we're putting in place, Minnie and I want someone in the top spot who really can understand and evaluate these new technologies as they come along. So we would be honored if you would accept the position."

Legend has it that Toby was so thrilled, she did cartwheels from one end of the R&D laboratory to the other. Serious scholars reject this, claiming that cartwheels, of the human gymnastic variety, were not conceived until tumblers appeared at the Circus Maximus in Rome a hundred years later.

But, hey, who's to say?

And what of Cassius the Closer?

It so happened that this very same day, after Max had returned to his office and was sitting in his chair deep in reverie, his assistant interrupted, saying, "Excuse me, Mr. Max, but there is this person outside who persuaded me to ask if you might have a few minutes to talk."

"And who might this be?"

"Cassius the Closer."

"Send him right in!"

Shortly, Cassius appeared—and behind him came a helper who wheeled into Max's office some sort of apparatus covered by a large red silk sheet.

"Cassius! Good to see you! How goes it? You know, I was going to send you an invitation to lunch next week. But the thing is, MaxImum's business has changed so much that, frankly, I don't see us doing a lot of work together in the future. Even so, we've

been very good for each other over the years, and I wanted to ex-
press my appreciation."

Cassius waved this off. "Not a problem! Indeed, it is I who
should be taking you to lunch, if you can spare the time. Selling
the Wheel, after all, was one of the greatest of my—nay, *our*—tri-
umphs. But, Max, as I'm here to show you, I have something even
better than the Wheel."

"Better?"

"Max, I'm going to ask you one question and one question
only: Can water run uphill?"

"Can water run uphill?" Max repeated. "Well, ah . . . no. Not
in my experience."

"Yes, it can!" said Cassius. "And I have the means to prove it
to you—right now!"

With that, he whipped aside the red silk sheet, revealing a barrel filled with water and, on a platform raised above it, an empty
bucket. Between the two was a device comprised of a thick tube,
inside of which (unseen) was a spirally wound sheet of copper
running the length of the tube. On the higher end of the pole was
a crank, which Cassius began turning.

"Observe and behold!" said Cassius, delivering a dramatic de-
scription of what he was accomplishing.

Sure enough, as Cassius turned the crank, water began moving
up the tube and splashed out the top into the bucket.

"Isn't . . . that . . . amazing!" said Cassius.

"Yes. Very."

"Max, this simple device—implemented on a larger scale, of
course—will revolutionize water delivery as we know it. At present,
any city or landowner not blessed with naturally flowing springs at
an appropriate location must send servants or laborers with buckets
to bring water to where it is needed. But this device can move water simply and easily and continuously!"

"Um . . . what's this called?" asked Max.

"This, Max, is the Screw."

"The Screw?"

"The Screw. Here's how it happened. I was on vacation in Sicily when I met this Greek guy named Archimedes. Friends introduced us at a party. Well, we got to talking and it suddenly dawned on me that this was the guy who calculated the value of pi. I mean, certifiable genius here! So I ask him about some of the practical stuff he's done, and he mentions this thing that helped his native Syracuse fend off the Romans during a siege. 'What might that be?' I ask. At which point, he says, 'The Screw . . .' "

And so another Wheel began its turn.

THE WHEEL OF SALES
A Summary

SELLING <u>YOUR</u> WHEELS

What about you? Your company? Your products? Your services? Your customers? What is *your* optimum selling style and strategy?

Every selling situation has a place on the Wheel of Sales, which is the sum of everything you have just read. On the following pages, we have organized the key points of the knowledge contained in the story and sorted them according to the four essential market types.

If you read carefully—and consider your own situation honestly—you should be able to recognize the characteristics in each category that apply to you and your company. If on every page you identify consistently with one of the four segments (it doesn't matter if it's closer, wizard, relationship builder, or captain and crew, as long as it's the same one), then—insofar as marketing and sales are concerned—you're probably doing things right. But beware: If you find variances from one page to the next—if, for instance, your customers are in, say, a captain-and-crew market, but you fancy yourself or your salespeople to be wizards—there could be problems now or very soon. Any mismatch is a possible red flag. Many famous companies run by well-paid people have made costly, and even ruinous, mistakes by straying from the selling style appropriate for the customers who pay the bills. By applying what you've learned here, you can be smarter than them!

Technology

2. FAST GROWTH

The technology advances, often dramatically and in big jumps. These advancements increase options and complexity.

The implementation of the technology is often custom-tailored to each buyer's special needs.

Though now more valuable to a broader range of people, the technology still has many skeptics.

3. INCREMENTAL GROWTH

The technology goes into widespread use. Market penetration increases and the technology becomes accepted by the majority of the potential market. Though it still continues to advance, improvements come in smaller, less dramatic steps.

Products become "feature rich" and options become a marketing tool.

Those who buy and use these products are familiar with performance issues and can hold informed conversations about them, often to the irritation of the dwindling number of holdouts.

1. BIRTH

The technology is new and revolutionary, yet primitive.

Products are capable of only basic tasks and have few, if any, features or options.

During this period of infancy, appeal and value are limited to a relatively small number of people—but, if the technology is successful, those few quickly become enthusiasts.

4. MATURITY

The technology is standardized and has near-universal acceptance within the culture. You're considered eccentric if you don't you use it.

Advancements are few and might be met with resistance. Choices of features and options diminish as they become standard to the essential product.

Products are simple to use, even "idiot-proof." But this causes the technology to become frozen—thereby creating opportunities for the next new technical wave that will force its obsolescence.

Customers

PROGRESSIVE CUSTOMERS

Want an advanced solution or capability. A higher level of performance. Are willing to risk the inconvenience and higher cost to get the performance gain.

Are buying state-of-the-art products that are custom-designed or tailored to the buyers' individual demands.

Are first-time buyers making a complicated purchase and need outside expertise from the salesperson to make the best decisions.

Example: managers with line responsibility buying the first generation of a high-tech system.

GATESWINGERS

Want to be the first. Want opportunity. Exclusivity. Ultra-high prestige. Unique moneymaking potential.

Are buying a one-of-a-kind product. A revolutionary technology. A service offered by nobody else on the planet.

Have no prior experience with what's being bought (because it's the first), but have the personal savvy or the resources to buy and make use of the product without extensive assistance on the part of the salesperson.

Examples: entrepreneurs and other visionary customers looking for fast-track opportunities.

RELATIONSHIP CUSTOMERS

Want a reliable, accepted product, but also want and need features and delivery options adjusted to their individual needs.

Are making a complex purchase and need help dealing with the complexity, but do not need unique design.

Are knowledgeable. They've been through it before. Customers are familiar with what they are buying and have definite opinions about what they need.

Examples: middle managers. Most of the business-to-business market. Consumer purchases involving an ongoing bond of trust.

WORLD CUSTOMERS

Want a standard product at a terrific price. No hassles. Quick purchases.

Are buying the products that everybody buys. They expect no special alterations to be made with respect to product or delivery.

Are very familiar with the product and need little if any help applying it to daily uses. The main reasons they want postsale service is if the product/service does not live up to expectations (defects, wrong size, other mistakes).

Examples: purchasing and administrative staff in the business world. Just about every consumer in the retail world.

Salespeople

WIZARD

Character: Confident. "Buttoned-down." Both a team player and a team leader. Professional demeanor and attire. Enjoys the challenge of creating unique solutions for each customer. Thrives on managing complexity.

Major Drives: Sees sales as a stepping-stone to a management position. Enjoys being at the center of things.

Important Skills: Needs to have very good organization and communication skills to deal with details and manage complex political relationships. Needs to be highly skilled at resolving objections.

CLOSER

Character: High energy. Extroverted. Charming, but also manipulative. Willing to do whatever it takes to close the sale whenever, wherever. Lifestyle: very upscale. Owns all the cool toys.

Major Drives: A big-time need to succeed. Too much money is almost enough. But also, in some, a genuine desire to change the world for the better.

Important Skills: Qualifying, presenting, resolving objections, closing. Has to be able to build a "dream" picture of the results of the purchase.

RELATIONSHIP BUILDER

Character: Solid citizen. Fun-loving. Likable. Hardworking. Good marriage. Civic-minded. Optimistic, but also pragmatic. Lifestyle is upscale, but not extravagant, despite a relatively high income. Likes a routine. Hates complexity.

Major Drives: Likes the entrepreneurial spirit of sales, but needs the security of an organization and a sense of belonging. Most prefer sales to management.

Important Skills: Resolving objections, closing; developing good customer relations and building repeat business. Has to have an inner sense that the customer always comes first.

CAPTAIN AND CREW

Character: Upbeat. Outgoing. Happy-go-lucky. Just average, everyday folks like you, the customer. Down-to-earth.

Major Drives: Satisfied with making a decent living. Not an overachiever. Works to make the money to have fun on days off.

Important Skills: All aspects of customer service. Must be able to handle "social fatigue" so as to withstand constant contact with the public.

Strategy

WIZARD

Market Opportunity: up to 20% of the total potential market.

Market Entry: You need cutting-edge technology that is developed and sophisticated. Expect a cool response from most prospects. Some will welcome the new capability you offer, but most will question the necessity of it or will object to the costs involved. Be prepared to reinvent the company every three to five years.

Core Selling Strategy: Knowledge is your most important asset. Apply that knowledge to create custom solutions and individualized systems for your customers.

RELATIONSHIP BUILDER

Market Opportunity: up to 70% of the total potential market.

Market Entry: Expect plenty of competition (especially of the "me, too" variety). The market has warmed up; lots of sellers want a piece of it. To succeed, look for a good niche others have overlooked.

Core Selling Strategy: Be your customer's strongest ally. Work for solid relationships based on creative problem solving, dependable delivery, personal attention to details, etc. Deliver added value through the sales force—and charge accordingly.

CLOSER

Market Opportunity: only 1% of the total potential market.

Market Entry: Expect an ice-cold reaction from most. But if you have the right product, the energy and the drive, and the capital to go the distance, this is an auspicious phase of the market cycle to start a business. You have little or no direct competition, and you can own the market for a time.

Core Selling Strategy: Build the dream. Play to the customer's fantasies and desires. Use excitement to conquer the customer's fear.

CAPTAIN AND CREW

Market Opportunity: up to 94% of the total market (remaining 6% are new entries, others who need extra support).

Market Entry: If you're entering the market with a new business at this point, expect a long, uphill battle against established competition. Usually this type of market is dominated by three or four major suppliers with organizations large enough to have economies of scale.

Core Selling Strategy: Make it easy to buy. Strive to eliminate barriers to the sale. Give customers low-price, easy-credit, no-hassles service.

Selling Approach

WIZARD

Each sale is complex and takes place over a number of months, not just one or two meetings. Typically, the sale is not to an individual, but to a group.

Buyer/Seller Relationship: None prior to the first sale, but during the project they will need to have a close working relationship. After the sale, the parties may go separate ways.

Style: Professional. Progressive. Instructive. Demonstrating technical savvy. Smooth when managing complexity—social and political, as well as technological.

CLOSER

The sale is simple, even though the item being sold may be exotic and high-priced. Time frame is immediate, with the sale taking place in one or two meetings.

Buyer/Seller Relationship: Typically, none prior to the sale—and often there is no post-sale relationship, either. Sell once and move on.

Style: High energy. Exciting. An evangelical enthusiasm. More than the product itself, you're selling a concept—a vision, a dream, a better tomorrow.

RELATIONSHIP BUILDER

The sale is a complex, involved process extending over a period of years. Sales here are not projects, but continue indefinitely, with one sale leading to the next.

Buyer/Seller Relationship: Significant. The seller has to have known the customer long enough that a mutual bond of trust has developed—even before the first sale is ever made.

Style: Warm. Friendly. A long-term approach. Demonstrating loyalty, ethics, attention to detail, a willingness to go the extra mile to get and keep the business.

CAPTAIN AND CREW

Each sale is simple, but the marketing relationship is extensive. Although the interaction between customer and salesperson can typically be measured in minutes, the marketing to win that customer might extend over years.

Buyer/Seller Relationship: The relationship with the individual salesperson is superficial; the real "relationship" is between the buyer and the brand.

Style: Helpful, courteous, efficient. The salesperson is there to make the buying experience easy, pleasant, and problem-free.

Marketing

WIZARD

Ideal Company Image: Smart. Progressive. Superior. Advanced technology. A team of experts to support you, the customer. Offering custom systems much better than the current standard.

To Generate Sales Leads: Offer free knowledge. Write bylined articles for professional journals. Mail reprints to prospects. Publicize technical accomplishments. Do speaking engagements. Do problem-solution-style advertising.

Qualifying Customers: You're often going to be dealing at multiple levels of the customer's organization. You need the right contacts at each level. Where you start depends upon what you're selling.

RELATIONSHIP BUILDER

Ideal Company Image: Tried and true. Years of experience. Established—but up to date, not old-fashioned. Champion of today's standard.

To Generate Sales Leads: Offer a free service. Use social networking to meet new prospects.

Qualifying Customers: The wizard looks for projects; the builder seeks accounts. Your goal is to identify the *best* customers, the ones who are going to give you repeat business month after month, year after year—enough to justify your time and attention.

CLOSER

Ideal Company Image: Avant-garde. Pioneering, progressive, the next wave. Polished. Well financed. Having the potential for megasuccess.

To Generate Sales Leads: Demonstrate the technology. Show the potential. Get a PR firm to create events for you. Make lots and lots of cold calls to get yourself in the door.

Qualifying Customers: You want the chief decision maker, someone who does not have to ask permission to authorize the sale.

CAPTAIN AND CREW

Ideal Company Image: Thrifty. Efficient. Offering quality at an unbeatably low price. Universal locations. The market dominator.

To Generate Sales Leads: Offer free product trials. Advertise. Use coupons and other price incentives. Deep-discount grand openings.

Qualifying Customers: Got a credit card? C'mon in!

Getting the Sale

WIZARD

Sales Presentations: Tend to be formal, sit-down, conference-room affairs. Good audiovisual aids and sales literature are a must.

Typical Objections: Does the benefit outweigh the cost and headaches of making a radical change? Is this design really the best solution?

Resolve By: Showing a realistic timetable for completion. Present data to demonstrate that the gain will be more than worth the pain.

Closing: Suggest a starting date. Send a letter of agreement. Recommend a smaller-scale pilot project to test performance and results.

RELATIONSHIP BUILDER

Sales Presentations: Might take place on the golf course or in a restaurant. Emphasize a superior delivery of the familiar, not the new. Show that you offer a better implementation of a standard solution.

Typical Objections: Tend to revolve around issues brought up by the customer's in-house experts—such as, "Can you meet our special specifications and delivery requirements?" Price is an issue, but not the most important one.

Resolve By: Supporting and working with the in-house experts; be an ally, not an enemy. Make adjustments to satisfy special needs.

Closing: Be there pronto when the customer needs you. Often, a handshake is all that is required to seal the deal.

CLOSER

Sales Presentations: Lavish, entertaining, exciting, sometimes even dramatic.

Typical Objections: "Should I spend so much money on something this new? Is this really going to get me the performance promised? Do I really need this gizmo at all?"

Resolve By: Showing that this new technology really works. Build the sense of tremendous opportunity. Sell the dream; skim past the details.

Closing: Ask for the sale immediately after the presentation. Offer a limited time for acceptance. Give "permission" to buy. Overall, inject a strong emotional push to people who are on the fence—either fear of loss or desire for fulfillment.

CAPTAIN AND CREW

Sales Presentations: Simple and short. An explanation of features and options. The more skilled salespeople are able to highlight aspects of importance to the individual customer.

Typical Objections: Is this the cheapest price? What happens if there is a problem after the sale?

Resolve By: Offering to meet or beat any other competitor's price. Offer money-back guarantees.

Closing: Help the customer feel comfortable with the decision to buy—emphasize return policies, price protection, etc. Highlight reasons for the customer to buy now. Make checkout easy.

Service

WIZARD

Great service means . . . total support. Doing whatever is necessary to provide results as promised. Taking measures to minimize disruptions to the customer's operations.

Keys to Repeat Business: The project nature inherent in this type of market often precludes a second sale. But where possible, you want to document performance so that management will approve a larger rollout of the technology. Suggest improvements that may lead to add-on sales. Forge good working relationships and look for *new* projects you can competently execute.

CLOSER

Great service means . . . a refund in the event of a major problem. Usually, the customer is self-reliant with respect to applying the technology, so service is not a determining factor for success.

Keys to Repeat Business: Often, there is no repeat business with the same customer.

RELATIONSHIP BUILDER

Great service means . . . being an advocate for your customer within your own organization. Being able to expedite an order when necessary, even if the reason for the rush is the customer's own fault. Not making mistakes, but resolving them quickly. Understanding each customer's individual preferences.

Keys to Repeat Business: Always deliver as promised, and work to build strong personal relationships within the customer's organization. Continuously look for ways to be of extra value to the customer. Maintain personal contact on a steady, regular basis.

CAPTAIN AND CREW

Great service means . . . no hassles. Fast delivery. Prompt exchange or money refund if the customer is dissatisfied. Policies empowering people who interface directly with the customer to bend the rules selectively when it will make a difference.

Keys to Repeat Business: Consistent quality and low price. Do everything possible not to lose 'em once you've got 'em. Keep the buying experience pleasant, easy, and problem-free. Try to make buying fun for the customer. Deliver friendly service, but keep each transaction efficient. Do everything you can to establish and maintain a buying habit with the customer.

THE FUTURE OF SALES
Afterword

Sales forces that are measurably World Class are few in number. The vast majority underperform their potential. Indeed, even as the corporate sales force has become an increasingly vital resource with respect to competitiveness, data from the 1990s show that there are tremendous opportunities for improvement.

For instance:

- Benchmark data revealed that only 5 percent of all sales forces were rated as "very good," which is the minimum rating to ensure customer loyalty.
- Even in the late 1990s, less than 10 percent of all sales organizations were objectively measured and evaluated on a continuous basis, with timely updates of data necessary to prompt improvements in performance and customer service.
- With respect to corporate culture, many companies continued to cling to the old-fashioned view that sales was an

entry-level position, and that the best performers would be promoted out of sales and into management.

- Some companies had not yet recognized that sales is a talent-based skill, one that most employees could never develop, no matter how much training they receive.

However, findings like these actually are good news to those companies willing to invest in the effectiveness of their sales organizations. Very simply, given product parity, if you improve the quality of your sales organization, and your competitors neglect theirs, you will win.

But the big question, particularly apt with the new millennium upon us, is: What will it take for a sales force to be World Class in the future? Everything described in the preceding pages certainly will continue to be the classic, time-tested foundation for building a quality sales force. Yet there is also a new trend emerging, one that will set the best apart from the rest in sales: the ability to make decisions based on "hard numbers"—that is, on empirical data, as opposed to intuitive hunches or subjective information.

By nature, most salespeople tend to deliver information in anecdotal form. They report to management what they have learned from talking to their customers. In the past, most market research has been subjective to a large degree, based on customer focus groups and opinion surveys, rather than on numerical data reflecting actual purchasing behavior.

Top sales managers today realize that you can't manage well what you don't constantly measure. What is probably the most important trend in sales is the increasing use of database technology to make better decisions. With the advent of the Internet and other computer networks, it has become possible to collect an enormous wealth of customer data and to sort it and analyze it faster and more thoroughly than ever before—and not just in consumer markets, where we've seen this trend emerging for some time, but now in business-to-business sales, as well.

As database technology becomes increasingly sophisticated, the best of the best in sales are using it to measure performance on a continuous basis. No longer is management obliged to make decisions based on last year's numbers. Management can get timely data, updated quarterly, monthly, weekly, even daily—whatever is meaningful to the individual situation.

Managers can track performance against customer-based criteria, and even more important, they can measure improvements in customer service by using disciplined methods very similar to the statistical-process quality-control methods and ISO standards that have dramatically affected the manufacturing world. In years to come, it's likely that the best and most desirable customers won't keep vendors who don't bother to track their own performance. It is even conceivable that larger, corporate customers may demand copies of the data in order to verify and review the quality of service they are receiving from the vendor's sales force.

Both now and in the future, the sales database is and will be an all-important tool. The technology can predict which factors will cause customers to buy—or to defect to a competitor. It can allow the sales manager to "drill down" to get information on specific salespeople and specific product orders and customers—or pull back to get a macro view of what is going on in the market. It can give you market share by an area as small as a ZIP code—and compare your performance against that of your competitors. It can also predict market trends, price elasticity, which features and options to bundle with the sale, and the life expectancy a new product or service will enjoy before it must be replaced by an upgraded model.

Max and Minnie—and everyone else until the last years of the twentieth century—never had it so good. In years ahead, the really smart sales organizations are going to keep the old values alive, but apply the new technology for all it's worth.

Acknowledgments

I would, first of all, very much like to thank Howard Stevens, my esteemed co-author, as well as Sally Stevens, his brilliant co-founder and wife; and the H. R. Chally Group for developing and making available the research upon which this book is based. The concepts they created from their empirical data collection and analysis are, I believe, absolutely fundamental to a valid understanding of customers, salespeople, and selling technique. My appreciation to those at Chally also extends to Don Kitzmiller and to Cheryl Gier for their practical assistance in a variety of matters.

Second, and almost as important, thanks—from all of us—go to the hundreds of thousands of salespeople, sales managers, customers, and others who have participated in Chally's research over the years. Your cooperation during the testing and interviews Chally conducted was nothing less than essential—not just to this book, but to the broader comprehension of what really works in sales.

I offer my personal and special thanks to Fred Hills, a terrific editor and certainly one of the best in the business, whose experience and lucid comments were genuinely appreciated. Thanks go as well to the capable and talented Sharon Friedman and Ralph Vicinanza for handling the business end of making this book a reality.

And big hugs to Hannah and David for leaving Daddy alone certain evenings and weekends while he was finishing this book—as well as to Sue for keeping them out of my hair, and for her unmitigated moral support and love.

One small caveat: Readers should note that I have compressed time in the story a bit more than might sometimes be the case. That is, I imply that the Wheel evolves from basic product to a universally accepted commodity over a mere matter of decades. With some products, like computers, that pace is not unrealistic, but for others the evolution is much slower. And, of course, it is unusual for a single company to survive and succeed over the entire continuum. Most of the smart companies that do achieve corporate longevity do so because they stick with a marketing and sales culture that works and instead switch products and technologies as conditions warrant. In the story, however, as it is dramatically ineffective to create a whole new set of characters every fifty pages, I chose to stick with Max and Minnie and have them stay the course.

Finally, it hardly needs to be pointed out that *Selling the Wheel* is a book about salespeople and marketing, not about history. Obviously, in telling my tale I have used considerable creative license with respect to the historical facts and have ignored many and rearranged others to suit my purposes. For instance, there is no evidence (none that I'm aware of, anyway) that wheels were ever used to build the pyramids of Egypt. If anyone is offended by my flagrant disregard of history (which is to say, if you can't take a joke), please accept my apologies.

My best to all of you.

Jeff Cox

ABOUT THE H. R. CHALLY GROUP

The H. R. Chally Group was founded in 1973 (originally, as SSS Consulting) and was funded by a grant from the United States Justice Department to develop a legally valid, actuarially based selection test for law enforcement officers. With the methodology developed for this test, it became possible to predict accurately a job candidate's future effectiveness in a particular line of work. At the conclusion of the Justice Department project, Chally began applying that methodology to what was then a neglected area: the assessment and selection of sales personnel.

Today, Chally serves more than two thousand clients, ranging from small and mid-sized companies to a considerable number of the Fortune 500. The firm offers a variety of services—employment and promotional testing, selection validation, sales productivity audits, customer and market audits, and sales and market strategy—as well as tools and aids to evaluate and improve corporate sales forces.

With funding from corporate sponsors, Chally conducts the research that determines the recipients of the World Class Sales Excellence Awards. On its own, Chally also applies fifteen percent of its annual budget to comprehensive but practical research about sales, sales management, and related topics. The sum of all this activity has yielded the leading database on sales benchmarking information.